Fields of
Glory

Fields of Glory

A Novel by Jean Rouaud

Translated from the French by
Ralph Manheim

ARCADE PUBLISHING • *New York*

First Arcade Paperback Edition 1993

Originally published in France
in 1990 by Les Editions de Minuit
under the title *Les champs d'honneur*.

Translated with the assistance of a
grant from the French Ministry of Culture.

The characters and events in this book are fictitious.
Any similarity to real persons, living or dead,
is coincidental and not intended by the author.

Library of Congress Cataloging-in-Publication Data
Rouaud, Jean.
    [Champs d'honneur. English]
    Fields of glory : a novel / by Jean Rouaud ; translated from the
French by Ralph Manheim. — 1st English-language ed.
        p.   cm.
    Translation of: Les champs d'honneur.
    ISBN 1-55970-165-X (hc)
    ISBN 1-55970-216-8 (pb)
    I. Title.
PQ2678.07677C413   1992
843'.914 — dc20   91-28975

Published in the United States by Arcade Publishing, Inc., New York,
by arrangement with Little, Brown and Company, Inc.

Distributed by Little, Brown and Company

10 9 8 7 6 5 4 3 2

Printed in the United States of America

TRANSLATOR'S NOTE

I wish to thank my friend Pierre Andler
for his invaluable help and advice in connection
with this exacting translation.

R.M.

I

SO IT WAS SIMPLY that these things always run in series, in dreary compliance with a system whose secret workings we were now suddenly discovering. An open secret, to be sure, from the very start. But each time so well covered over that now, when it burst upon us once again, it hit us like a hammer, leaving us dazed, stunned with grief. Grandfather was merely the final blow, as if to tell us, quite needlessly: Now-get-this-into-your-heads-once-and-for-all. Rubbing it in as if we hadn't learned our lesson. This was just too much and might well have gone unnoticed. One afternoon, without the slightest warning, his heart stopped beating. Of course his age may have had something to do with it, but at seventy-six he hardly showed his age. Or perhaps recent events had marked him more than one might have thought. A secretive old man, aloof, almost absent. There was something Chinese not only in his detachment but also in the extreme refinement of his dress and manners. And in his features as well: small slit eyes, eyebrows angled like the roof of a pagoda, a sallow complexion that owed less to any Asian ancestry (which could only have been exceedingly remote, a by-product of invasions, a genetic quirk) than to overindulgence in cigarettes, a rare brand that we never saw anyone else smoking — almond-green packets with old-fashioned lettering. Once when we asked him, he claimed to order them from Russia, but on another occasion he said, with the same deadpan expression, from Rangoon beyond the moon. Production, I am certain, was stopped at his death. All by himself he smoked up whole fields of tobacco, lighting each new cigarette from

the butt of its predecessor, a manipulation which, when he
was driving, threw his 2CV into an improvised rodeo act.
Squeezing the butt between the thumb and forefinger of his
right hand, holding the new cigarette in one corner of his
mouth, he would concentrate his attention on the incandes-
cent tip in utter disregard of the road, lightly touching the
one to the other several times and taking methodical little
puffs until a frail thread of smoke arose from the point of
contact. Then, throwing back his head to avoid being
blinded, soon surrounded by a dense cloud that he waved
away with the back of his hand, he would raise the hinged
window with his elbow, briskly toss away the butt without
so much as a glance at the road, and give the wheel an
arbitrary jerk that would jolt his passengers in all direc-
tions. Was his intelligence blunted by old age, or was he,
after a long and perilous life, lulled by a certain sense of
immunity? Toward the end there were not many who dared
ride with him. My teenage cousins had the bright idea (this
happened two or three times; we didn't see them very often)
of tying a scarf or a tie borrowed from their father around
their heads and shouting a kamikaze's banzai when driving
off with him. We, on the street, would respond to their
farewells by waving handkerchiefs and wiping away imaginary tears. Actually, we all knew they were in no great
danger, because the car was incapable of much speed. Still,
the experience — Grandfather's persistent crossing of center lines, his way of trespassing on the left side of the road,
or skidding and bouncing over soft shoulders, not to mention his unpredictable procedure at intersections — left his
passengers as green about the gills as would a ride on a
roller coaster.

In delicate situations there was no point in offering one's
services by gesturing and signaling. The rather absurd pan-

tomime of turning an imaginary steering wheel in empty space could even be interpreted as resentment at not being in the driver's seat oneself. And with Grandfather there seemed to be no point in anything we could do. It was useless to warn him, to tell him in sign language that the obstacle behind us was only a few centimeters away; he'd look at us wearily through the smoke of his cigarette and wait calmly for his bumpers to convey the same message. With this routine, the car body was damaged all over, the mudguards bent, the doors out of alignment. We had nicknamed the car Bumpy. If Grandfather ever found out, his indifference prevented him from showing it; in all likelihood he had secretly catalogued us once and for all as little snotnoses or something of the sort. Maybe he really didn't care.

When it was raining, a far from unusual state of affairs on the Atlantic coast, the 2CV, buffeted by the gale, panting against the wind, shipping water on every side, made you think of a dilapidated fishing smack which, in disregard of the weather forecast, had ventured out on a stormy sea. The rain beat down on the canvas top, the fragility of which we sensed with alarm, and the rolling thunder resounded in our little cabin like a reminder of the deep seas. Seeping first through one, then several microscopic holes in the canvas, droplets formed on the underside; these soon expanded, trembled, divided, and fell vertically on a head, an arm, a knee, or, if no one was sitting there, on the hollow of a seat, where, swollen with rivulets, they would form a small puddle that we had to remember to wipe up before sitting down. The water-clock effect soon gave way to acute torment when the infuriating regularity of the dripping was exacerbated by unforeseen splashes from the side. The rain trickled through the half-demolished stripping of the doors — oh, that innocent-looking drizzle, which in the long run will soak you just as thoroughly as a downpour. At first we would try to remain, like Grandfather, undaunted by the storm, to break the mystery barrier and prove that "all this" (his occasional weary, disenchanted expression) was only a set of prejudices and that rain was a mere idea, an accident, a shimmer of the universal illusion. This may be true at the highest spiritual level, when the body detaches itself from matter and rises into the air — or in one of those comfortable, silent, watertight cars that make you feel you're riding in the middle of a cloud — but after a certain number of kilometers this gentle fizzing, which picked up the rust of the doors and deposited tiny spots on the seats, imposed its obstinate rhythm, and after some minutes of damp yoga, convinced by brute reality, you resigned yourself to taking out your handkerchief and wiping your face. It is the tyranny of such stubborn little realities that little by little consigns childhood to the slow decomposition of all living matter.

Strangely enough, after the first irritation the oblique trajectories of the droplets made for an atmosphere of good humor; our disappointed expectation of the miracle that would make the rain slide off us as off a duck's back suggested a jocose way of getting even. Quickly, briskly, or landing softly at the end of their flight, the droplets would fall haphazardly on the corner of an eye, a temple, a cheekbone, or aim straight for the hollow of an ear; in any case they would be so unforeseeable, with such complex parameters, that the only possible way of avoiding them would have been to hide your head in a sack. Our game, a rudimentary version of battleships, consisted simply in announcing "Touché" when one of these drops, more forceful than the rest, gave us a start and left us with the feeling of being the target of an unknown marksman. The only rule was not to overdo it, not to collapse in the seat or make a show of unbearable pain over a harmless drop of water. Disputes were frequent but mild. We were careful not to raise our voices; Grandfather's 2CV was a place of solemnity — the interior, that is, for when seen from outside, the state of its body was too lamentable for that.

Once, just once, Grandfather joined in our game, when a drop transformed the tip of his nose into a dripping candle. Breaking out of his usual silence, he exclaimed in the kind of hoarse, muffled voice that comes from someone who seldom speaks, "Nose sunk."* We immediately stopped squabbling, almost shocked for a moment by this intrusion of a grown-up into our gang. But once recovered from our surprise we took it as good news, the return of an elderly prodigal son: Grandfather was not so far away, he was within reach of our games, though we had supposed him at the far end of old age, deep in a clutter of remote memories. Relieved, perhaps, to show how heavily his absence had weighed on us, we burst into a joyful laugh, half disguised by our delayed comprehension of his pun. This running, sinking nose provided an ideal conclusion to our battle at a time when, unable to bring it to an end, we were reduced to monotonous repetition of the same silly routine. It proved definitively impossible to resume our improvised rain game, as though Grandfather's quiet exclamation had exhausted its possibilities. On the other hand, it long served us as a rueful comment on various domestic disasters: the milk that had boiled over, the flashlight battery that had given out, the bicycle chain that had come off, the watch that had

---

* Untranslatable pun: The same French verb denotes a *sinking* ship and a *running* nose.

stopped. It even extended to the individuals responsible: Papa's nose was "sunk" when he ran out of gas two kilometers from town after trying to make it by zigzagging and thus using up every last drop of gas in the tank. Since he traveled a lot, the locution might, if he had lived, been taken into the language. And in a hundred years great ingenuity would be needed to trace its origin.

In the Lower Loire, rain is a life companion. It gives the region, which is otherwise rather nondescript, a characteristic style. Clouds charged with ocean mist plunge into the Loire estuary near Saint-Nazaire, follow the river upstream, and like an endless bucket chain empty their excess humidity on the Nantes area. The actual amount of water cannot bear comparison with the monsoon rains, but is distributed so evenly over the whole year that in the minds of casual visitors, who are not always favored with a break in the clouds, the region's reputation for overcast skies and rain is soon established. It is hard to undeceive them, even by pointing out the legendary mildness of the climate — witness the mimosa in the backcountry and, here and there in the gardens of leading citizens, a dog-eared palm tree — because the statistics on precipitation and hours of sunshine speak for themselves. Undeniably it's a damp climate, but in the end you get used to it. Under a persistent drizzle you swear in all seriousness that it's not raining. Wearers of glasses wipe the rain off them twenty times a day without thinking, get used to walking behind a constellation of droplets that diffract and break up the landscape, creating a gigantic kaleidoscope in which, unable to take bearings, they let themselves be guided by memory. But at nightfall, when a gentle rain descends on the town and the neon signs come on, inscribing their luminous calligraphy in the blue-black night, those little dancing stars that glitter before your eyes, those blue, red, green, and yellow sparks that splatter your glasses, suggest the son et lumière at Versailles. And how dull the original seems by comparison when you take off your glasses.

Consequently, opticians do a good business. Not that there is more myopia here than anywhere else. But the more often you wipe your glasses with a shirt tail drawn furtively out of your trousers, the corner of the tablecloth in a restaurant, or an unused area of your handkerchief, the greater the likelihood that your glasses will come apart, fall, and break. That is one of the many drawbacks of rainy weather, along with a persistent sadness and the splitting headaches induced by screwing up the eyes. This crawling sensation at the roots of your hair may have another cause, but who is to blame if you are forced to take shelter in the cafés along your way? What can you do but wait with a drink, then two or three, for the sky to clear? Standing at the bar, silent, absorbed in his reflection in the window, the listless drinker watches the stooped passersby holding up their collars as they hurry along under the downpour. No trace of a supercilious smile when he sees an umbrella blown inside out. He merely congratulates himself on having had the good sense to take shelter. A slight letup in the rain, a barely perceptible brightening of the sky, and he concludes that the weather has taken a turn for the better, downs his *petit vin blanc,* buttons his coat, hunches up his shoulders, and is on the point of going out, but no, it's pouring again. Without wasting a word, he points at his empty glass: the same . . .

There are sure signs of impending rain: a brisk west wind, gulls flying far inland and coming to rest like balls of absorbent cotton on plowed fields, in summer, swallows grazing the rooftops and silently, watchfully, circling over gardens, foliage rustling in the wind, the frenzy of the little round leaves, men looking up at the dappled sky, women taking in armfuls of washing (oh, those incomparable

sheets, dried in the sea wind with its homeopathic particles
of salt and iodine) and leaving on the line clothespins as
multicolored as a cageful of tropical birds, mothers calling
home their children who have been playing in the sand, cats
passing their paws behind their ears, and, in response to the
tap of your fingernail on the glass, the downward jerk of the
barometer needle.

The first drops are imperceptible. You look up, unwilling to believe that anything can have fallen from that luminous pearl-gray sky, shot through with flashes from the
distant ocean. The fine rain is often content to accompany
the rising tide (in times of neap tide with a coefficient of fifty
or sixty) in its twice-daily routine. We always tend to think
of the grandiose equinoctial tides that so terrified Phoeni-
cian mariners — the sea sinking away from under a ship's
bow, as if to feed the great waterfall at the end of the earth,
and returning in mountainous waves to recapture lost
ground — but these are exceptions that occur only twice a
year. Ordinarily, this moving in and out over a stretch of
mud and rock strewn with seaweed attracts little attention.
The undifferentiated sea and sky take on an ash-gray tinge,
long veins of anthracite delineate the waves and clouds, the
horizon is no longer a dividing line between the elements,
but a kind of continuous porridge. Rain has taken over the
whole countryside; it can come from the trees or the grass,
from the gray asphalt attuned to the sky and the sadness of
the people. An endemic sadness, expressing itself with
economy, now and then overflowing through abuse of
wine: glasses accumulated in clumsy attempts to open the
Northwest Passage leading to joy. Rain is the alchemist's
quest for the philosophers' stone. Rain is inescapable. On
sensing the first symptoms, you hold out your hand. At first
you feel nothing. You hold it palm upward, the skin of the

palm is more sensitive. But what do you catch? A pinhead, a
tiny lens revealing a field of clouds, a miniature sky at the
end of a finger, comparable to Mont-Saint-Michel or the
basilica at Lourdes seen through the peephole in an old-
fashioned penholder. With this rudimentary droplet in
hand, you ponder the likelihood of a change for the worse.
Sometimes there is no change. It won't rain. The rising of
the tide is accompanied only by a caressing, silky wind that
brings more order than turmoil to your hair and has little to
say of the ocean. Or, in negative terms, it speaks of an
apathetic Sargasso Sea, of Bermudean doldrums. The coast
of Brittany is laved by the Gulf Stream, that pirate river
carrying tepid water from the Caribbean to the Atlantic to
which we owe our mimosa, our oleanders and geraniums,
even if we cheat a bit by bringing our flowerpots indoors in
the cold season. Without the Gulf Stream the estuary would
be frozen solid in winter like the Saint Lawrence, since the
latitude of Nantes is the same as that of Montreal. And
snow in this region is no more than a manner of speaking, a
light film every ten years that melts as soon as it falls. Apart
from the famous winter of 1929, when Pierre went to
Commercy, and the winter of '56, which was fatal to so
many homeless persons but enabled the children of the
estuary to pose proudly with a snowman they had made —
having as they had read but had hitherto been unable to
verify lumps of coal for eyes and a carrot for a nose, with
hat, pipe, and scarf completing the panoply. And then the
drought of '76, when not a single drop of water fell on
Brittany, when the fields were sere, the corn bore ears no
thicker than lupin flowers, and the cows had no more flesh
on their bones than greyhounds — a meteorological freak
attributed, for want of a more plausible explanation, to
some sort of mysterious sunspots, to the eruption of a

volcano in the southern hemisphere, or the wobbling of the earth on its axis. Such things are remembered precisely because they are not the norm. The norm is rain. When rain falls with the rising tide, it is, strictly speaking, not rain. It is powdered water, a bit of meditative music, an homage to ennui. There is a kindness in the way it caresses your face, smoothes out the creases in your forehead, rests it from worrisome thoughts. It falls discreetly, you don't see it, windowpanes do not preserve its imprint, the ground absorbs it without suffering harm.

Ennui, on the contrary, is a poison of the soul. Oh, the ennui of interminable drizzle, the low sky — low enough to rub shoulders with steeples, water towers, and pylons, to mingle with the tops of tall trees. We oughtn't to make fun of the early Celts for fearing that it would fall: metaphysical heavens are invented under high azure skies; here, the sky is a slate covering that weighs heavily on the region, sparing only a thin layer between the clouds and the dark, waterlogged earth. This unbroken drizzle of the black months of November and December is no longer rain; it is a thoroughgoing invasion, a slow, dense, obstinate curtain, that needs no more than a light breeze to penetrate sanctuaries where the dusty ground has preserved its light color; it permeates the entire countryside and crushes the last stirring of hope in the hearts of men. You feel that the world is coming slowly to an end, sinking into the muck, that instead of the final fiery explosion announced by the religions of the desert, you are witnessing a vast program of dilution. Not here those big puddles resulting from storms and dried up by the first sun, nor those sudden floods necessitating emergency evacuation, victims rescued by rowboat from the upper stories of their houses (the fields along the Loire are often flooded, but the river, it must be admitted, is entitled to its variable geometry). The decor seems intact, except that the country is greener, a deep knapsack green, while the city is grayer, a leaden gray. The spirit of the marshes has taken over. Under their greening the meadows and lawns conceal sponges. If you venture over them, your shoes pick up enormous soles of mud. Take care not to slip if you stroll beside gullies or ponds; don't go too near the bushes — you'll be in for a shower — or lean against a tree — the bark is sticky. Playing Hercules, you break great rotten branches. Those heavy blue jackets don't dry overnight. The bread is soggy, the walls are saturated with damp, continents form on the wallpaper, and you wonder how this microdampness managed to get in. The radiators heat up in vain; the water passes as easily through the eye of a needle as through a triumphal arch. Your body creaks in every joint, your bones reactivate ancient aches. Long dreary days without so much as a hope of clearing. The lights stay on from morning till night. Now and then you push the curtains aside to make sure that the rain is still falling as persistently, as conscientiously as ever, without ever seeming to let up. The most fragile succumb; it's toward the end of the black months that people jump into wells.

This drizzle lacks the rhythmic richness of the downpour that rebounds with a clink from window ledges, gurgles in gutters, and, always in a hopping-skipping mood, beats against the roof with the obstinacy of a piano tuner, so that a practiced ear can distinguish what the roof is made of: houses north of the Loire are most often roofed with slate, the outbuildings with tile, sheds with wood and corrugated iron. After the squall that ends the tempest, a dome of mercury trembles over the city, whose contours under the bright, silvery light are marked with the precision of an engraver: the stone curlicues on the steeples of Saint-Nicolas, the leaves of the trees, the quill feathers of high-flying birds, the broken line of the roofs, the bird-friendly aerials. Sharpened vision enables you to read a signpost a hundred yards away or recognize, and hence avoid, an approaching bore. The sidewalks gleam blue like the bellies of the sardines on sale at corner stalls in season. The buses whish past with a muffled sound, splashing delicate white spray from under their tires. The well-washed shop windows are resplendent, the treetops are haloed with millions of silver nails, the air is as fresh as a peppermint drop. The city rests like a memory in the translucence of a crystal bell.

The intention of the spring storms is to make a clean sweep. If the cold weather persists, they wait for the next moon, then they sweep away the whole wintry mess with gale-force winds. Sometimes in their enthusiasm they carry off one tree and decapitate another, a car is overturned, chimneys take leave of their moorings, weathervanes vanish. After all, a stupendous force is not easily regulated; something is bound to go wrong. It would be an exaggeration to speak of a cyclone, even if now and then a wind gauge jams or a dike succumbs to the fury of the waves.

The northwest wind brings a glacial rain that sets the blood tingling. It buffets you on the slant. Your face is lashed with iron filings, watery needles pierce you and stun you. Your cheeks, nose, hands, turn tomato-red. The ideal of beauty has changed from romantic pallor to tropical sunburn, but blotches have never been regarded as emblems of seduction — not even among the American Indians, who demand a coppery red. Yet, though they do not provide a beauty treatment, at least these winter rains give you the sense of well-being that comes of strenuous effort when, back home again and dried and swathed in flannel,

you listen to the howling and clanking of the tempest outside. An innocent pleasure, from which unfortunately some
are excluded: the homeless and the indigent. Poverty gets
no good out of anything. Diogenes, the source of the myth
about beggar-philosophers, lived under clement skies.
Great as Alexander may have been, one might conceivably
bid him get out of one's sunlight — but what can you do
about clouds? The Cynic wouldn't have lasted very long in
his tub around here; frozen stiff, wet to the skin, without
the least ray of sunshine to warm his old bones, he would
no doubt have appealed to the Salvation Army for help. To
the poor the winter rains are a scourge. The winter rains
haven't the whimsical quality of spring showers, when you
prudently scrutinize the sky before going out, and find it
serene, wrinkled with little clouds scudding at high speed,
in a hurry to cross the country and counter an invasion of
barbarian rains from the east. Confidently, you leave your
umbrella in the cloakroom or what serves the purpose: a
wastepaper basket, a drum of washing powder. So fervent
is the longing for spring after the dark months that, on the
strength of the deeply ingrained belief that if swallows
make the summer it is because of their plumage, we rebel
against winter outfits. True enough, the first signs are there,
mild, fragrant breezes season the still wintry air, the days
are beginning to get longer, as you can tell by certain reliable indications: the light at office-leaving and shop-closing
time, the new timetable, the streetlamps coming on too
early. You are so absorbed in this good news, so delighted
by the perceptible approach of spring, that you fail to notice
the sudden darkening of the sky. And then abruptly, without a word of warning, the rain comes down. It falls with a
comic alacrity, an almost infantile deluge with a quick,
joyful sound, a kind of trial gallop, a show of fireworks in

broad daylight. You have only to cross the street: a few steps farther on the pavement is dry. You run to take shelter under a balcony or a shop awning; you huddle in a doorway with some other people. You smile at one another despite your dripping hair; no one takes this rain amiss. It's not rain, it's a game of hide-and-seek; a game of cat-and-mouse. Actually, we have barely caught our breath when the sky recovers its azure mood. A break in the clouds and all is forgiven.

Grandmother thought these rains were stupid. In her opinion, it should rain once and for all and get it over with. Her idea of a rain schedule was as follows: she set aside eight days in the year, during which the amount of water now distributed over twelve months would fall, and divided the rest of the year into a (not too) hot season and a (not too) cold season. Instead, this Breton uncertainty, this perpetual rain and shine. She railed against bad weather as against all other mishaps. Twenty times a day, despite her implacable principles, she would utter a *nom de nom* (whose name we never found out) full of menace and sinister implications. More than a simple invective, it seemed to cast doubt on the world order, and though she never named the guilty party, it was clear that he was not very far away.

Her marriage to Grandfather had been arranged, if not imposed, by their parents — a triumphal union of well-to-do business families, condemning their descendants to a golden takeover.

The couple's business success was short-lived, swept away by the convulsions of the era, but in the euphoria of their "Contented Ladies" clothing store they had every reason for confidence, and for fear of imperiling their future the betrothed pair arranged to love each other. Not that love is all that important; after thirty or forty years all couples are in pretty much the same situation. But once the disagreeable feeling that you have not been master of your fate sets in, it's not easy to convince yourself that a different start would have made no difference. You are left with the suspicion that something better may have been lost forever. It's only the intolerable that you don't forget.

Her wedding had been the crucial date in Grandmother's life, so much so that it represented a kind of year zero, the basis for all determination of before and after, comparable to the birth of Christ and the founding of Rome. When we speculated about her age (most often to marvel at her longevity and impressive stamina), one of us always argued that the solution was simple: you just had to remember that she was married in 1912 at the age of twenty-five — as though this event, more than her birth, marked the dividing line at the base of all time reckoning. Clearly she herself had determined this benchmark. Who else could have done so? Certainly not the privileged witness to the event, one year younger than herself, our taciturn grandfather. But the calculation proved so complicated when the dates did not end in 2 that Grandmother's age had become "twenty-five in 1912," a fossilized age impervious to the passage of time. We aimed at no more than a rough estimate of her age, based on the apparent state of her health and the amount of time elapsed since that date, a variable flux, which stagnated during the years when we detected no change in her, and suddenly speeded up when we discerned some unmistakable symptom of old age — hardness of hearing, dragging feet, lapses of memory, frequent repetition of the same stories. But apart from her very last days, when she held a hand in front of her mouth and did her best to speak softly for fear of being overheard by the head nurse — who, she said, hid behind the wall radiator and prevented her from going out to dance in the evening — it was a grandmother–great-grandmother aged twenty-five in 1912 who died at the age of almost a hundred while cracking a last joke, an elegant pirouette that made her daughters laugh through their tears.

As for their golden wedding anniversary, we had all calculated correctly — it was simple. There had been talk of a great family reunion, a banquet accompanied by entertainments, each one of us doing a turn, and a play, in preparation for which Papa and Lucie, my mother's younger sister, worked up a scene from *La Jalousie du Barbouillé*, whose text they had found in a faded edition of the Larousse classics. There would have been a dance, for which Grandfather would have dug out his violin and reconstituted a flute and string quartet with his old friends from the Nantes Conservatory, but whether because the flutist had breathed his last or, more likely, because these velleities had succumbed to the family's Jansenist mentality, the summer ended without their so much as setting a date. The vacations of the various members refused to coincide. And before long it was too late: autumn, and the rains, came, the family members dispersed, and in the following year, with its additional ounce of gold, calculation became impossible. We promised to meet again at future anniversaries. Of what kind we couldn't have said — platinum or diamond? A discussion (cotton, china) that ended up with the marriages of Chiffon and Figaro. A propos of which Lucie flung her soprano voice into Cherubino's aria "Voi che sapete che cosa è amor," and we all applauded.

To the aged pair the failure of our plans undoubtedly came as a relief, a great bother avoided. The idea of the quartet had aroused no enthusiasm in Grandfather, who more and more preferred silence to music. From then on the violin remained in its case, and if he tinkled the piano keys now and then, it can be put down to a kind of magnetism —

it is hard to go near a piano without uncovering the keyboard. But he didn't keep at it for long: a few bars of a
fugue, an aria, the theme of a sonata. He would stop in the
middle of an arpeggio, sit for a few moments with his hands
on his knees, dwelling on the unfinished phrase, then carefully put the green silk scarf back on the keyboard. Toward
the end he contented himself with a single note, as though
to take the measure of the silence, and later still there
wouldn't even be a note, but only a silent caress of the
ivory keys.

Grandmother, for her part, flew into a rage when our
cousins spoke of decorating the 2CV with streamers and
ribbons on the festive day and daubing HAPPY ANNIVERSARY
on the rounded trunk. She made it plain that she would
have nothing to do with any shenanigans. In general, the
2CV was a permanent bone of contention between Grandfather and her. Not that she found fault with its humble
mien. Their financial status had long been unequal to the
resplendent cars they might have driven in their days of
prosperity. A woman of strong character, she stood up
under adversity and, as long as her principles were safe,
attached little importance to the visible trappings of wealth.
She had harsh words for those who let themselves be taken
in, such as the unfortunate young man who bragged about
the speed of his sports car. "Too bad," she said, "that it's
gone before we have time to see it." Without loss of dignity
she had moved from the large ornate house of tufa, brick,
and wood, with its successive additions, its half-landings,
and its rooms opening out on roof terraces, to a dark,
cramped, ground-floor apartment in Riancé. She, who
called down every known curse on the manufacturer of a
fountain pen that refused to write, showed no sign of dejection at having to give up almost all her furniture. In the

bedroom the piano was right next to the foot of the bed and
seldom free of encumbrance. That may have had something
to do with Grandfather's loss of interest in it, for to open it
he had to sweep away a pile of clothing. What with the
bedside table and another small table, movement became
impossible when the cupboard doors were open. The move
from thirteen rooms to two meant parting not only with the
accumulation of a lifetime but also with the bequests of
earlier generations. More than asceticism, it was a sweeping away of memory.

Still, it was Grandmother's recollection of this past that
drove her to keep two or three heirlooms, in particular a
cumbersome, poorly designed worktable, when she could
have kept the attractive mahogany bookcase with the oval
glass panes in the same space and to better advantage. But
this worktable was her mother, her grandmother, herself,
and every industrious woman in the family — it was a stele.
She disposed of the rest with a detachment that was not
always shared by her husband. He gratified us with the
sullen look that differed from his usual taciturnity only by
its more ostentatious way of saying nothing. Not that he,
any more than his wife, was overly attached to the goods of
this world, witness his stays in the monastery of La
Melleraye and his association with the Trappists. And if he
remained exigent in vestmental matters, it was because his
past as a tailor had given him a feeling for cut and an eye for
workmanship, for properly creased trousers, light, supple
material, and expensive lining — after all, Il poverello, the
draper's son Francis of Assisi, who can hardly be suspected
of frivolity, asked to be buried in a winding sheet of gray
cloth. What irritated Grandfather was having to be present
when things were being given away. And yet the beneficiary
daughters all showed the utmost tact. If there were any

feelings of offense, jealousy, or disappointment, they were well suppressed. Each insisted on offering her gift to the others before accepting it. And if one, with infinite precautions, expressed her desire for a particular one of these heirlooms, the others hastened to assure her that it didn't interest them in the least. The result was an accumulation of petty resentments that oozed out on the occasion of a visit, when one of the daughters caught sight in the house of another an object she had coveted: "Hmm, Mama's lamp looks just lovely on your dressing table."

The 2CV is the skull of a primate: windshield eyes, radiator nose, sunshade eyebrows, engine prognathous jaw, while the roof equals the slightly convex parietal bones. Nothing is lacking, not even the protruding cerebellum, the trunk at the back. Grandfather was the solitary immobile surveyor of this abode of thought. Grandmother felt excluded from it; indeed, she preferred to walk rather than let him drive her, at least for short distances. And walking was not her forte; it was made hard for her by the aftereffects of a difficult delivery, a tear that left her with a swaying gait. When Grandfather took the wheel of another car, she had no objection to getting in beside him. She found charm in all cars but the 2CV. In her opinion, it was not adapted to the North Atlantic climate. What was the point of the removable canvas top if the weather was never right? Not to mention this raging, whirling, fatiguing wind. Every attempt to take the top down on one of the rare fine days was a battle with rusted metal corroded by the salt air, frozen joints, and stiff, cracked canvas that refused to be rolled up. To make matters worse, you could never be sure that ten kilometers farther on you wouldn't have to put it back up again in a frantic hurry. Grandmother had decided once and for all that this so-called cabriolet had no business north of the forty-fifth parallel. To cross deserts, climb the Ahaggar Mountains, as the young people were doing these days, it was just the thing, but the Lower Loire was something else again.

Her main grievance was the 2CV's unfitness for rainy weather. A third source of leaks after the top and the doors was the rudimentary ventilating system, a simple, close-meshed grille three fingers wide at the foot of the windshield, covered by a sliding shutter, which, especially after the rubber gaskets had rotted, was not quite watertight. Even in dry weather the wind whistling through the grille got on Grandmother's nerves. How could anyone be expected to keep calm with that incessant spitting? She welcomed the first little drops with I-told-you-so sighs, for they confirmed the soundness of her convictions, and wriggled in her seat as though trying to dodge them without incommoding others with her troubles. Then, in the face of Grandfather's impassivity, she set about caulking the seams with old rags that were kept in the "glove compartment" (a shelf under the dashboard). She took hold of them with her fingertips, complained about their filth (they served interchangeably to wipe the dipstick and the windshield, and even, when a presentable corner could be found, to polish the tips of Grandfather's shoes), rolled them up, and tried to wedge them against the glass, but they fell at the first jolt. A few *nom de noms* and she'd try again, sponging and keeping it up all through the trip. Grandfather remained imperturbable.

Since he was driving very slowly, the windshield wipers, which were geared to the engine, moved at the speed of a slug in millimetric jerks. Now and then they would jam, and Grandfather would punch the windshield to make them resume their slow semicircular movement. They painted muddy fans on the windshield, exactly the opposite of the desired effect. Annoyed that no one but herself seemed aware of the danger, Grandmother rubbed the inside of the windshield with an anxious hand that, starting from a center on a level with the eyes, described wider and wider and flatter and flatter circles and timidly encroached on the

driver's side, just enough for him to see the difference —
and thanks to the gap thus obtained in the thin film of
condensation, thanks to this direct view of the state of the
windshield, it became obvious that one couldn't see a thing.
Since the wipers were obviously to blame, Grandmother
grabbed hold of the lever with which they could be oper-
ated manually from the inside and turned it vigorously, all
the while reviling them. This hyperactivity of the wiper
blades, this sudden change of speed, this accelerated rigid-
ity, had something of a silent film about it: two workmen
lazily shoveling, two dishwashers dawdling over a stack of
plates, suddenly springing into action at the sight of the
tyrannical foreman. But the result nevertheless suggested
slovenly dishwashing: a gelatinous magma, coated with
half-moons and impervious to vision. Then in a fury she
would lift up the hinged side window, which inevitably
fell back on her elbow, stick out her arm, and, with the help
of the rag, admit a narrow fillet of light. The sudden
emergence of the swiftly moving road, of the trees alongside
it, of the milky splashes of the rain pelting down on the
asphalt, was the revelation of an enveloping universe, in
which the closed world of the 2CV was encased. Though
Grandmother's arm was not long enough to wipe the whole
windshield, her view through her cleared porthole enabled
her at least to instruct the pilot to keep to the right and gave
her the authority to yell "Watch out" at the passage of an
enormous truck, whose suction sufficed to rock the frail
skiff.

Driving blind did not trouble Grandfather. Huddled in
his seat, his hands on the lower part of the wheel, a cigarette
quietly burning away between his lips, only his hat visible
to passersby. Constant exposure to nicotine had yellowed
the top of one eyebrow. This unusual yellow amidst the

irrepressible invasion of white suggested a last flare-up of youth, a strategic retreat of life into this sulfurous point. In conjunction with the other, immaculate, eyebrow, it made for an asymmetry suggesting a trace of hemiplegia in the old man's face, an impression accentuated by the fixity of the half-closed right eye, stung by the smoke, which he blinked now and then, throwing his mustache off center and giving it a Chaplinesque look. He seemed so absorbed, so far away, that he might have been asleep. Sometimes he actually was, a state of affairs that had earned him a number of mishaps — a wheel in the ditch, a torn-off mudguard. Grazing the upper arc of the wheel, his gaze lost itself in contemplation of an imaginary blue line traversing miles and miles of thought in which there was obviously little room for us. His secret garden, said Grandmother. An admission that she feared to get lost if ever she ventured into it.

His only confidant was the gatekeeper at the abbey of La Melleraye, a little monk with an infinitely gentle smile and a tongue so glib that, barring an order from his superior, he would never for all the world have exchanged his position for his brothers' rule of silence. On busy days such as Easter Sunday he would run from group to group, welcoming new arrivals with open arms, shaking hands, with a sign of recognition and a kind word for everyone. He would pat children on the head, pressing them — a little too tightly perhaps — against his habit with its unpleasant smell of mold, and ask the older ones about their schoolwork; and if it came to his ears that one of them was not exactly a shining light in Latin, oh well, in the first place he, the gatekeeper, was not in charge of Latin studies, and, come to think of it, why should anyone wear himself out studying a dead language that only a few old men like himself understood. After thus assuring himself at little cost of popularity with backward pupils, he would raise his clasped hands heavenward as though asking forgiveness for his near-blasphemy. This voluntary recluse reproached himself for his loving nature.

Much as he enjoyed his conversations with this one and that one, he would cut them short the moment he heard the gentle chugging of the 2CV — which he could identify from among a hundred other vehicles — and hurry out to welcome his dear Monsieur Burgaud. Grandfather went to see him twice a week. He would bring home one of the abbey's succulent cheeses with its orange-tinged crust, the cheese itself being straw-colored, smooth and firm, shot through with little pinholes. The flavor of that cheese has no doubt been forgotten, regretted by none, because no one has ever heard of it. And along with it dozens of delicious little satoris have no doubt evaporated.

The two would stroll together in the portion of the park reserved for visitors (women were admitted only to the gatehouse, where the products of the monastery were on display). The crunching of their steps on the gravel walks could be heard from far off. They walked slowly, halted at moments of excitement in their dialogue, then started off again: the frail little monk in his rough brown habit, Grandfather hardly taller, bent forward, his hands crossed behind his back. They spoke softly, as respectful under the great centuries-old trees of the sanctity of the place as under the white vault of the Cistercian chapel with its pillars of pink granite. The monk accompanied his words with ample flourishes of his sleeves — his way of raising his voice without encroaching on the silence. Weather permitting, they would make a ritual stop halfway, sit down on the rim of the fountain, and silently contemplate the calm surface of the water. But this foretaste of eternity was not to the gatekeeper's liking; he would have ample opportunity for silence when visiting hours were over, and his way of kicking pebbles with the tip of his sandal made it plain enough that he was impatient to resume the discussion.

On hearing the news of Grandfather's death he burst into tears — the spontaneous grief of an afflicted child — but quickly recovered his composure. Wiping his tears on his wide sleeve as though in a farewell poem, he asked my forgiveness: "I'm sure you understand. I've lost my best friend." After the customary condolences, he once again, forcing himself a little, displayed his perpetual smile, that façade of beatitude which led visitors to say that despite

the stern rules of the monastery the monks were undoubtedly the happiest of men. Did they miss women? Of course
not, said the gentlemen, they didn't know how lucky they
were. "Good riddance," the wives joked. Everyone had
said what was expected of him, and there the discussion
ended.

Brother Eustache had been surprised at my grandfather's failure to come and see him lately. Except during
the summer holidays it was unusual for him to stay away so
long, and his prolonged absence seemed to augur no good.
The monk remembered the time when my grandfather and
Madame Burgaud had spent several weeks at the house of
their younger daughter after the death of her husband —
only forty, wasn't he? — leaving her with three young children. That had been only six months before. What terrible
trials God sometimes sent, the meanders of his love were
not always easy to follow. On his return, Monsieur Burgaud seemed to have aged. Sunken cheeks, sharpened features, he had lost interest in their discussions and answered
beside the point or not at all. His thoughts were far away.
The death of this beloved young man preoccupied him and
he kept coming back to it. As though discovering belatedly
that all life is rooted in that dark source. He often ques-
tioned his friend about "all that," and the little monk
would reply with an evasive gesture encompassing the chapel, the trees, the clouds, and the fountain.

Little by little, Brother Eustache came to speak of their
interminable conversations and automatically started to
walk, drawing our silent group along with him. What had
they talked about? Oh, about everything. Music, of course,
but not exclusively — very little, come to think of it. He
himself had only a vague idea of anything more modern
than Gregorian chant, and though they were of one mind

about Bach, they were far from seeing eye to eye about Wagner, whose music bored him, the monk, to tears, not to mention those pretentious libretti. No, to tell the truth they philosophized, though the term may be a little excessive for amateurs. Monsieur Burgaud had been a man of open mind, alive with curiosity, perhaps a bit too Cartesian, but this reservation was compensated for by his extreme attentiveness to others. The world and its ills — that was what most of their discussions were about. Once they arrived at a diagnosis, they tried to work out formulas for a better future. They had even — time had elapsed, he could speak of it now — sent a letter, after throwing away any number of drafts, to the president of the republic, calling on him to set up what they called "charity sweep-up vans" (a term probably borrowed from the Tour de France and definitely not contributed by my grandfather, who all his life had disdained the world of sports). The idea was to send out a fleet of pickup trucks all over the country to succor and if need be shelter the indigent.

This revelation did not have the expected effect on us, for we knew that Grandfather had been corresponding of late with the highest state dignitaries, a sign that with advancing years he had ceased to be impressed by earthly glory. We tapped our foreheads and put him down as "eccentric." The secretariat of the Elysée Palace had assured him by return mail that his letter had been forwarded to the relevant department.

Brother Eustache had let his friend talk him into it, and blushed to look back on their presumption. Oh dear, that was him all over. The little monk shook his head, raised his eyes to heaven, and smiled beatifically. He had ceased to grieve, for he saw Grandfather among the angels.

The longer he spoke, the more evident it became that he was performing a kind of transplant, which consisted in removing Grandfather from his family and taking possession of him for himself. Remarks like "What, you didn't know?" or "Monsieur Burgaud didn't tell you?" that accompanied his stories reinforced him in his role of "elective affinity," as contrasted with imposed kin, the implication being that we had failed to appreciate this great man, that he alone had recognized his greatness and therefore had every right to monopolize his memory. In a sense, the little monk was right. In him Grandfather had found an attentive ear, an echo to his own secret preoccupations. His visits to the abbey had served as a pretext for salutary escapades. We had long known that his silences hummed with feverish thoughts. As the consoler of his last days, Brother Eustache had gathered the honey. We forgave him and thought it fitting and proper that he should come into this inheritance.

Yes, yes, but he was keeping all the good grain and leaving us the chaff. Far from the world and its temptations, Brother Eustache had only a fragmentary vision of life. Only high-grade confidences, generous thoughts, lofty mystical impulses were admitted into the reserved precinct of the abbey. It was a purified Grandfather who entered into this rough sketch of the heavenly Jerusalem. He set down his human burden on the threshold and displayed his divine face within. We knew more than the little monk about everything else connected with my grandfather, and his image of the saintly man needed a bit of retouching: Grandfather hiding his sweets to avoid sharing them with us, or at

Christmas giving us a miserable pittance, which Grandmother would increase tenfold behind his back. And I was
sure he hadn't boasted to the monk of last summer's escapade.

Every summer since their retirement he and Grandmother had visited their daughter Lucie in the Midi. After a
first exhausting trip in the 2CV, punctuated by repeated
breakdowns and disappointing hotels, Grandmother put
her foot down: the train was quicker and more reliable and
that was that. The comments of impatient motorists on the
slowness of their vehicle — why weren't they in the old
people's home or the cemetery, where they belonged —
stuck in her craw. It was true that they weren't as young as
they used to be, as they themselves agreed when they got off
the train, put down their four heavy suitcases on the platform, and stood there, dead tired, their faces marked with
fine lines deposited by the smoke of the locomotive, Grandfather mopping his forehead below his panama hat, Grandmother fanning herself with yesterday's awkwardly folded
newspaper. While John, Lucie's English husband, picks up
the suitcases and carries them to a baggage truck, while the
little group heads at the snail's pace imposed by the old
people for the impeccably blue sky at the exit, they all argue
whether, in view of the travelers' fatigue, it wouldn't be
better to come by way of Lyons, despite the need to change
trains and the three hours' wait, rather than by the direct
line via Bordeaux with its innumerable stops. In Grandmother's opinion it's six of one and half a dozen of the
other, and she fails to see why no one has thought of
dynamiting the Massif Central and cutting straight across.
She swears that next time she will bring a little pocket
atomizer to freshen her face; perhaps that will help her
to forget that she is traveling in what she cannot help

calling a cattle car. The food smells (imagine, people peeling hard-boiled eggs right under her nose), mingled with the stench of sweat. The heat is no excuse. That leads to a commentary on hygiene and the lack of it: some people start the day smelling bad; the half-moons under their armpits date from the day before. But what she deplores most of all is the free and easy ways. At the start of the trip their neighbors behave as if they had stepped out of the château (meaning, of course, the château of Riancé, seat of one of the oldest families in France): affected elegance, crossed legs, hand over mouth to cover a ridiculous little cough, exaggerated civility attendant on lifting a suitcase onto the baggage rack; then, as the kilometers pass, they step on one another's feet, lecture one another presumptuously on good manners — the French garden runs wild. Never, she had sworn long ago, would she be caught dozing with her legs apart and her mouth open. And she fans herself more vigorously than ever, as though to blow away all trace of that terrible night amid the sweet scents of Provence.

Mister Djon, as the Arab farm workers call him, drives slowly on the first hairpin bends of Les Maures with the windows down and his forearm resting on the sill. He feels that the fragrant air of the hill country, that miraculous open-air kitchen, is already beginning to make up to the old couple for the misery of their journey. The dense, heady smells of sage, thyme, marjoram, rosemary, basil, and mint when the car rubs against them, the resinous scent of the conifers, the bitter fragrance of boxwood, the bittersweet aroma of the fig trees, the stripped wood of the cork trees, the gnarled trunks of the olive trees, the silvery sheen of holly leaves, the varnished smoothness of the laurel, the ocher earth, black schist, a sky veering to indigo framing the green of the pines, and, invading the hollows in the conversation, the loud, obsessive song of the cicadas.

Climbing, the travelers enter into the coolness of the northern slope, where oaks and beeches thrive, only to plunge back at the end of the loop into the crushing brightness of the Midi. The old people give in to the motion, sway gently on the curves, and express their gratitude in the gaze they turn toward the summits.

Grandmother is sitting in front beside the driver. Possession of an English son-in-law shows that her life has not been conventional. She told her daughter simply: "I shall call him Jeannot." Fearing to make herself ridiculous by mispronouncing the foreign name, she chose a radical solution. It seems likely that Jeannot-John loves her for the vanity that is this strong woman's weakness. She is one of the few people who bring a smile to his hollow cheeks. She concludes the story of her tribulations on a comic note: the obscene, and to her intolerable, movement with which some women try to create a draft in their underclothes. She takes her skirt between two fingers, raises it slightly, and shakes it as though to remove the dust. Success. Good humor is established, an encore seems justified. She repeats her number. The disagreeable impressions of the journey are forgotten when the pink roughcast of the house appears at the end of the gravel drive, whose entrance is marked by two cypress trees. Grandfather's wicker chair awaits him in the shade of the big locust tree. There he will spend the summer.

Early each morning he took possession of the chair after a short walk in the hills, amid the coolness and subtle scents of the dawn and the blissful silence preceding the tumult of the cicadas — a distance hardly exceeding the circuit of the house, but which he covered attentively, giving a name to every plant and every butterfly, at least to those identified in the color plates of the *Grand Larousse Encyclopédique*. Not that he was interested in botany — the garden of his house in Riancé was a great jumble — but he had devised this subterfuge as a means of communicating with his grandchildren. Leading one of them by the hand, he would point his cane at a plant, announce simply, "Savory," and relapse into his mute reverie. In thus playing the naturalist and transmitting knowledge, he felt that he was fulfilling his educational duty. It was useless to ask any more of him, least of all, as Lucie suggested, that he should teach the children to read music and play the piano a little. He affected not to hear. A Beethoven deaf to little Mozarts.

Returning from his walk, clad in a white sports shirt and duck trousers, he settles down in his easy chair. The morning is spent reading the paper and starting crossword puzzles (that Lucie finishes in bed at night), tracing a geometric figure centered on himself in the dust with the tip of his cane, and, still with his cane — a flexible bamboo from his son-in-law's collection — building small pyramids of dry leaves or deflecting the course of a column of ants. Pulling his panama lower with the mounting intensity of the light, he looks about, lifts his hat in reply to the distant greeting of a field hand. No one passes on the road leading to the vineyards and the cork plantation without showing him a small mark of allegiance. In the eyes of these active people, this replica of an impassive old Chinese under his tree is a symbol of superior wisdom. Grandfather is the axis around which the house revolves. When a worker whose tractor has broken down comes looking for Mister Djon, it is grandfather who indicates the direction in which to look for him. Or if John is in the house, grandfather assumes the role of messenger: "Jeannot, they're looking for you. The tractor again." Stopped by the brim of his hat, the smoke of his cigarette comes to rest for a moment before enveloping him in an evanescent halo. In the midst of his reverie, a cylinder of cigarette ash falls on his duck trousers. He takes his memorandum book (where among other things he notes his botanical discoveries) out of his shirt pocket, delicately slips the cardboard cover under the cigarette ash, and slides it intact into the ashtray that rests beside him on a log. Grandmother, who finds it scandalous that he should derive so much prestige from doing nothing, brings him a basket of broad beans to shell. If she's knitting, she makes him hold the skein while she winds the wool. Much of the time, provided he's not expected to get up from his chair, he is admirably docile; he even puts up with his daughter's scolding when he has been so thoughtless as to toss a still-burning cigarette into the parched grass and an infuriated Lucie stamps on the offending butt, very much like Saint George stamping on the dragon's neck. As if this were not sufficient, she points out the charred stumps on the hillside, the gruesome aftermath of last summer's hellfire, when the roaring barrage of flames was stopped less than two hundred meters from the house, describes a night lit up by thousands of fires as though an army had been bivouacking on the hill, the plaintive crackling of wood, the smell like

that of burned toast in the early morning, and now this
mound of desolation — all very likely brought about by a
cigarette like this one. After which grandfather repents as
though he had set the match to Joan of Arc's pyre.

Exactly, says a triumphant Grandmother (who happens
to be passing), she's told him a thousand times if she's told
him once that he'd be the death of us all with his cigarettes,
and resumes her stroll in the wake of little Lucas, Lucie's
youngest, who persists in going about nude and runs away
howling when she tries to slip him into the little blue swimming trunks she has ready for him. They will come back
soon in the same order if wee little Lucas has not been
caught, the child still howling, golden brown from top to
toe, his penis, which is much too short to wobble, sticking
out like a dowel. Tempted for a moment to take refuge with
his grandfather, he changes course at the last moment,
remembering his repugnance for the names of flowers and
butterflies, a rejection of knowledge that has earned him a
kind of disgrace. Actually, Grandfather takes no part in the
drama that the child, to judge by the volume of his tears,
considers one of the world's injustices. He affects an Orien-
tal indifference that puts one in mind of those Zen monks
who show their disciples the way to perfect emptiness by
wringing the necks of kittens. (How does the kitten feel
about it?)

Grandfather abandons his lookout post for lunch and
the long siesta that follows in the heat of the afternoon,
when the angry air quivers as though struck by a
flamethrower. He comes back for the tea ceremony, Grandmother's concession to her English host in return for the
change of name she has imposed on him — which obliges
her to forgo her habitual café au lait. Later, in the cool of
the evening, interminable games of boules are played before

his eyes on the carefully swept terrace. When disputes occur, the players ceremoniously borrow his cane to measure
distances, and he becomes the arbiter whose mere presence
suffices to ensure fairness. At nightfall a cloud of mosqui-
toes drives our Saint Louis of the boules players away from
his tree.

One morning his chair remained empty.

The advancing forenoon brought Grandmother strolling
around the locust tree. The early risers had taken Grandfather's absence as a welcome breach of the ritual. Grandmother showed discreet signs of anxiety. "Hasn't Alphonse
come back from his walk?" or "You haven't seen my husband?" She even solicited the help of wee little nude Lucas,
the perfect scout, thanks to his wanderings up hill and
down dale, but sensing a trap, he fled as fast as his legs
could carry him. Grandmother in hot pursuit tried to
explain the misunderstanding: "I only wanted you to find
Grandfather for me," but he, twice burned, refused to listen: If it's not to put on his trunks it must be for some kind
of lesson. By noon, all inquiries having proved fruitless,
everyone was thoroughly alarmed.

In vain John had covered his father-in-law's usual morning itinerary, circled the house, gone a little way down the
hill behind it, passed through the cork trees, skirted the dry,
reed-edged watercourse, traversed the vineyards and the
scrubland to the south, where the old man acquired most of
his botanical lore. Grandmother feared the worst. She had
visions of Grandfather, who had never been able to distinguish between parsley and carrot tops, wandering off the
path in search of his infernal plants. She saw him fainting in
the bush or bitten by a snake, too weak to call for help, his
leg turning black, attacked by the monstrous finger-thick
bees known in those parts as "bombs," whose sting is fatal,

or laid low by his diabetes, which no one took seriously and which ordinarily responded to a treatment consisting of three lumps of sugar in his morning coffee and plenty of candy throughout the day, but which, now reactivated by the summer heat, was poisoning his blood and urine; she saw Grandfather in a semicoma, unwinding the film of his life, lying on a bed of aromatic herbs, looking up at a dizzy-blue sky, an inverted pit that seemed to be inviting him to plunge into it; she saw him breathing his last in the arms of his betrothed of 1912, spelling out rockrose, myrtle, and thistle in an apotheosis of violins and cicadas.

All the field hands, former *harkis* for the most part, were mobilized and put their hearts into the search, for Monsieur Burgaud had had a kind word for every one of them. Grandmother urged them to beat the bushes, to sound the cisterns, to explore disused trails, keep their eyes open, and above all, if they found that Alphonse had been bitten by a snake, not to make him walk, because that would speed up his circulation with fatal consequences. They should call for help, serum would be brought to him, every member of the search party should carry a whistle, a trumpet, a drum, he should let loose with the cry of the muezzin or the shout of the woodcutter, and precious seconds would be gained. She divided the estate into four zones and the men into four groups. It was she who directed operations, only occasionally consulting John, who contented himself with approving. The men advanced in a line, spread out like beaters. There were several hunters of wild boar, authentic Hurons of Provence, who claimed to know every square inch of terrain for miles around and assured Grandmother, "Don't worry, Madame Burgaud, we'll bring back your husband."

They brought back nothing at all. At three o'clock the

last group returned empty-handed. It was a ticklish business in the forest-fire season, but since things had been quiet in the last few days and the mistral had died down, John called in the fire brigade.

The red jeeps and the first-aid truck were lined up Indian file in the drive. A little man in a hat and light-colored suit passed them in review, intrigued by the imposing lineup. As a special favor in view of his advanced age, the bus has let him off near the two cypress trees marking the entrance. The cigarette dangling from his lips is only half consumed, but after one look at the fire fighters he puts it out without delay and stuffs it into his jacket pocket. With his bamboo cane he lifts a corner of the tarpaulin covering a stretcher, which fortunately is unoccupied. Something seems to be going on in front of the house. The long table of the grape harvesters has been set up. Empty glasses have imprinted pink rings on the wood, which glitter in the afternoon sun. Not far away the fire chief is talking with a small group of volunteers. All are looking up at the hills in the distance, following the finger of a man in heavy black leather. Consequently no one notices the new arrival, who joins them, listens, and, taking advantage of a silence, inquires, "Has there been a fire?"

It was almost seven o'clock. A group of ten volunteers under the leadership of a fire chief had just found Grandfather.

When he realized that all the stir was on his account, he slipped into the house and shut himself up in his room. Certain members of the search party, who would have liked to know for what purpose they had wasted their afternoon, thought his conduct a bit cavalier. John felt the time had come to open a second demijohn of rosé. Already, explanations were being found for the old man's befuddlement.

Similar cases of amnesia were remembered, people picked
up far from home who'd forgotten their own names: physi-
cal or emotional shock, softening of the brain, stroke.
In their eagerness to get to the bottom of the old man's
amnesia, the family could hardly wait for all the people to
go home.

Suspecting that she herself would get nothing out of him,
Grandmother had sent her daughter, but Lucie had to
pound on his door for quite some time before he consented
to open it. He claimed to have spent the day at Hyères,
specifically in the garden of exotic plants. After exhausting
the resources of the maquis, he had felt the need to broaden
his knowledge by familiarizing himself with the natural
phenomena of other regions, especially the flora of the
tropics, and sure enough he had seen marvels: the banyan
tree with its aerial roots, the giant sequoia of California,
named after an Indian chief, the flamboyant with its epony-
mous fiery crown. He proceeded to run through a long list
of botanical curiosities and then, for fear of overdoing it,
stopped short on a note of irritation: Was there any law
against taking a little trip? No, they all agreed, there was no
law, but next time couldn't he let them know? Or did he
have something to hide? And if so what else but a woman?
That is, in the coded language of our thoughts, a scheming
woman, obviously endowed with every charm, whereas
Grandmother was a horse of a different color, desirable no
doubt in the flush of youth, since there is always a certain
charm in freshness, but even in the oldest pictures never
pretty — and now an old squaw with her dislocated hip,
her faded complexion, her shapeless body that she hid
under a purposely shapeless dress. A fund of imagination
would be needed to find a place for love in that body —
whereas that other woman in Hyères, younger no doubt or

at least endowed with that imperishable something, the slender ankle, for example, that often defies the ravages of time, the unblemished youth that often graces the feet of old ladies, that tiny bone with its precious covering of taut skin which, if a man conscientiously, religiously concentrates all his desires upon it, might enable him to love the same woman as long as he lives. But Grandmother's thick ankles are always, even in the torrid heat, encased in heavy nylon stockings of a mouse-gray–violet tinge, because like those blind, pigmentless animals that live in deep caves where the light never penetrates, she is determined to protect the whiteness of her legs, the immaculate milkiness of her body. How can she hope to compete with the mystery woman of Hyères, whose body had been conditioned by half a century of sea bathing?

The answer came next day when Grandmother looked through the pockets of his jacket. Yesterday's hero had taken his place under the acacia as though nothing were amiss. Ordinarily he would have asked to have the harvesters' table removed from his field of vision, but esteeming no doubt that no good could come of calling attention to himself, he said nothing and contented himself with moving his chair. Curiosity about the vineyard and the cork plantation seemed to be at its height, to judge by the unusual number of passersby on the road. Grandfather answered every greeting, apparently untroubled by the sly smiles of those who inquired after his health. Most of the men had joined in the search parties and didn't seem to hold it against him. Monsieur Burgaud was back at his lookout post, life resumed its course, and he, the thread of his private reveries.

Not for anything in the world would Grandmother have wanted it thought that she was in the habit of searching her husband's pockets. That was not her way. But you have to consider the circumstances, and beyond a doubt Grandfather's preposterous explanations gave ground for a suspicion that was to prove entirely justified. Grandmother showed Lucie a small rectangle of pink cardboard, a ticket showing date and destination and irrefutably putting the finger on Grandfather's escapade, a return ticket to — but rather than pronounce the terrible words, she gave Lucie the ticket to read: Ile du Levant, the nudist paradise.

It was so often pointed out from the shore: the mythical isle, the scandalous island, the third to the east after Porquerolles and Port-Cros, so fervently longed for in secret that no one felt entitled to cast the first stone at Grandfather. Actually, the news was received with delight. He was admired for his courage. Nothing should have surprised us in such a man: his independent mind, his solitary expeditions, his insouciance at the wheel of his car. If any one of us was to take this trip, it had to be him. We visualized him inspecting the island with an air of detachment, of preciosity as it were, drawing on his cigarette while screwing up his eyes to take in the nudity of the women, the multiform breasts, the quivering flesh, savoring the golden-brown skin perfumed with suntan oil, and on the boat coming back, as the island receded in the distance, memorizing the fish stories he was preparing for us: the aerial roots, the fiery crowns — there, to be sure, we felt he was going too far. But his escapade left us wondering. As if the old man had been tacitly given license to make the best of what was left to him of life. After this, it even seemed to us that if he chanced to survive Grandmother he might remarry, like the old friend of his apprenticeship years in Paris, when the two of them, aged twenty and penniless, attended concerts free of charge by serving in the claque —

well, anyway, this friend, after a brief widowerhood, had just remarried. Though described by the groom as "youngish," the bride had been all of fifty, but even so his old friend's marriage might well have put ideas into the head of a grandfather suddenly released from his vows of 1912.

Grandmother wanted no fuss. She asked us not to discuss the affair with anyone and not to let on to Grandfather that we knew. Less than a year later, as it turned out, as though to prove that he had been right to fulfill his old dream of Cytherea before it was too late, Grandfather died, convinced that he was taking his secret with him. It happened one night — it was his heart, in their little room so overcrowded that the piano had to be moved out before the coffin could be brought in . . . the heart, of course.

II

*W*HEN IT WAS THE TURN of our diminutive aunt, there was nothing to it. The drip tubes were removed from her emaciated arms as they rested submissively on the sheet beside her mummified body, the feeding tube was pulled out of her nose, and her brave heart offered no resistance. In three seconds it was all over. Her small white head drooped to one side.

Under similar circumstances a miracle of obstinacy has been known to occur; on its own initiative, the organism ventures a perilous survival trick. It may not capitulate for years, sometimes as many as twenty, during which its vegetative life takes refuge in the extremities: the nails and hair. Such obstinacy would have been in keeping with my aunt's nature; hadn't we seen her struggling for hours to solve by arithmetic an algebraic problem that would have submitted without difficulty to one or two well-conceived equations? But the honor of an old teacher was at stake. She wasn't going to listen to any presumptuous young whippersnappers who thought they could impose on her because they were in high school now. No doubt it was this obstinacy that had enabled her to live through her three weeks' coma.

To the whole town she was Aunt Marie, a local variant of the little father of the people. The curé of Random, whose zealous helper she had been, began his funeral oration by saying, "Our Aunt Marie has left us." The Bossuet-like tone annoyed us. The whole town, after all, wasn't feeling the same sort of grief. As a matter of fact, she had had only two nephews, Father and his cousin Rémi, the sons, respectively, of her brothers Pierre and Emile. It was

Pierre who had had the little cottage in our garden built for her without bothering his head over the land register or a building permit. He had done it to save his sister from the chicanery she suffered at the hands of the austere nuns in charge of the school, which had lodged her until then. But it had also been a way, after the ravages of the Great War, of consolidating what was left of the family.

By then it was unlikely that she would marry, if she had ever intended to. What men had escaped the massacre found no favor in her eyes, or she in theirs. Her little two-room hermitage was the exact counterpart of her ascetic life: a rudimentary kitchen (her only specialty was a sticky, lumpy white sauce, but as a rule three or four walnuts were sufficient nourishment for her shrunken body) and a bedroom, hardly more spacious, furnished with a bed, a washstand, a cupboard, and a light-elm chest of drawers with a glassed-in bookcase on it, in which she kept her schoolbooks and a few religious works, and a prie-dieu — all of which pathetic, valueless belongings were carried away after her death by a junk dealer called in by Rémi.

The bare white walls accentuated the pietistic atmosphere of the place. To them were affixed what in our aunt's mind constituted her theological Trinity: a crucifix, behind the head of which she had slipped a sprig of box blessed on Palm Sunday, renewed each year (the box tree in our garden provided the whole town with its fronds, a fact of which we were more than a little proud), and, facing it, two impressive engravings of Our Lady of Lourdes and of Saint Theresa of Lisieux.

On the occasion of the centenary of the apparition at Lourdes an international competition was organized (the prize being an eight-day pilgrimage) and our little aunt had won hands down: she was unbeatable on questions about the discharge of the *gave de Pau,* the dimensions of the Massabielle grotto, and the color of Bernadette's eyes. From her journey she had brought back this portrait of the Virgin, inscribed like a diploma with her name and rank: first among millions of participants — like a safe conduct to heaven.

In the lower left-hand corner the little shepherd girl is kneeling beside the spring, her wretched skirt spread out in the grass, her head covered with a scapular, a rosary imprisoned in her clasped hands. She raises her luminous face toward the tall white lady haloed in silvery dust, who smiles at her from the top of her rock, as elegant as a high-fashion model, her waist delineated by a silky blue scarf whose folds cling to the line of her thighs. For in spite of her ethereal look, this Immaculate Conception conceals beneath her tunic a body full of grace. To convince oneself of this one need only start from the bare feet that peer out from under the hem (the slight slope of the rock acts as a heel), follow the long legs, the narrow hips, the flat bosom (Our Lady of Lourdes does not give suck), graze the long swan's neck, and emerge from the clear spring of the eyes as they gaze lovingly at the ecstatic child. Mystery of Incarnation. This is my body. Our Lady of Lourdes is the most beautiful of Virgins, at least of the myriad Virgins figuring in the visions of peasant folk and providing such lovely place names as Notre Dame du Bon Secours, de Toutes-Aides, de la Peinière, de la Salette, who long ago severed the cord attaching them to the original Virgin — unmarried mother, that young woman of Galilee beloved of the Holy Ghost.

The glory of Lourdes has been somewhat eclipsed by the rise in prestige of the saint in the black and gilt frame on the opposite wall, the newly canonized Theresa. Her credit has been enormous since she saved the cathedral of Lisieux from the bombardments of 1944 — the church standing alone among the ruins seems to prefigure the neutron bomb. One of those would have spared the houses roundabout, but for the period the saint's achievement wasn't bad.

In the photos, Monsieur Martin's daughter has a round Norman face, with apple-red cheeks. But the Sulpician artist, with his sense of the universal, effaced these local singularities in favor of a sugary-pretty little thing, hugging her legendary rosebush as a champion bicycle racer might his trophy. Behind her head, surmounted by the coif of the Carmelite nuns, a halo of mat gold forms a perfect circle, the center of which is situated in the middle of her forehead. The saint appears as in a medium shot; the artist has truncated her body — perhaps he was suspicious of feet. You can give a face a look of perfect innocence, lengthen the waist, flatten the breasts, plane down the hips, but the sexiness of the instep is beyond your control. Thus face-lifted, fully recovered from her consumption, the Little Sister of the Christ child is all set to perform her miracles.

Our aunt kept a tiny snippet of cloth, five millimeters square, which had touched the saint's clothing. Armed with this viaticum, she felt confident of disarming all those nasty fevers. When one of us three was sick, she would take advantage of a moment when Mother left the room to make us kiss her scrap of cloth and sponge our forehead with it, thus gathering up a microdrop of the perspiration in which the essence of the disease is thought to be concentrated. Zizou, the youngest, doesn't give a damn; Nina, the eldest, objects, but her feverish, semicomatose state gives our faith healer a free hand. Then she goes to get Mother and tries to persuade her to take our temperature again. Thoroughly exasperated, Mother tells her that a fever of 102° doesn't come down in five minutes. Aunt Marie insists. She finds it hard to believe that a piece of cloth that might have touched the body of Saint Theresa is less effective than aspirin.

The saint of Lisieux has overshadowed numerous ancient glories, pillars of the sacristy — not, to be sure, the most austere, Teresa of Avila, John of the Cross, Catherine of Siena, Dominic, those seekers of light amid the dark night of the soul — but such saints for domestic use (whose efficacy has, however, been confirmed time and time again): as Cornelius, Christopher, Antony of Padua, Barbara, Eloi, Joseph, and of course Victor, our local saint. Our aunt had built up a card file, something on the order of the Grand Albert, a collection of esoteric recipes much used in rural districts. All the blesseds, those saints-to-be, were listed and many holy pictures classified. A prefatory catalogue of terrifying symptoms refers the reader to the saint specializing in the corresponding disorder. The work of a lifetime.

Hors concours, the Savior offered to the world his glorious heart, extracted without incision from his chest in the manner practiced by the Filipino shamans. With the daring modesty of a young girl uncovering her breasts, the Lord opens his shirt to show the Cross planted between the auricles, thus prolonging the sufferings of the Passion until the end of time. His powdered complexion, his Louis the Thirteenth hairdo, make Black Friday seem infinitely remote. The prayer on the back of the picture promises thousands of days of indulgence to those who read it. For the Sacred Heart is concerned first and foremost with the salvation of the soul. Coming to specific problems, for "intestines" (pain) you are referred to Saint Mamertus, for "glaucoma" to Saint Clara, for "blindness" to Saint Lucia,

for "hornets" to Saint Friard, for "Saxon pirates" (possibly
tourists) to Saint Similien, for "wolf" (encountering a) to
Saint Francis, for "justice" to Saint Yves, for "infants"
to Saint Nonne, for "orphans" to Father Brottier, for
"brothers" (friendly understanding among) to Saints Do-
natien and Rogatien, for "marriage" to Saint Barbara, and
for "drought" to Saint Vio, who in the Lower Loire department did not ordinarily have to be prayed to for very long.
Under "pig," it goes without saying, we find Saint Antony
and his temptations, but also a certain Saint Gourin. Deep
in the forests of old Armorica, a wild boar charged the
venerable hermit. And Saint Gourin cried out, "Beware,
piglet. In attacking Gourin you've made a big mistake."
Flabbergasted, the beast lay down submissively at the feet
of its new master. Ordinarily when a boar became trouble-
some, the recommended procedure was to repeat those
words while walking three times around its wallow. Our
aunt, however, thought it preferable to make pâté of its
flesh. She was inclined to classify Saint Gourin and others
like him as "dubious," for she thought it essential to distinguish between heathen wonders and the Christian message.
She was determined to owe her miracles exclusively to the
Catholic, Apostolic, and Roman church, and not to any
avatars of those so-called Celtic gods, Belen and Gargan.
Father liked to tease her by saying, "Scratch Saint Michael
and you'll find Mercury." She shrugged her shoulders dis-
dainfully, but we felt that these amalgams shook her a little.

When mothers came to see her about their children's
schoolwork, they would take advantage of her card file.
They would discuss bad marks in dictation or arithmetic,
attribute scholastic backwardness to dental problems, and
leave with a prayer to Saint Fiacre. On the other hand, there
was nothing to be gained by praying to Saint Colomban,

whom some people implore to confer a spark of intelligence on their slow-witted children, for our aunt relied upon the excellence of her teaching methods to fill the gaps. That was her rationalistic side.

When necessary, if prayer proved ineffectual, she added a poem of her own:

> Saint Christopher, before you ford
> This river with the child on board
> Take heed that he is like to grow
> As heavy as the people's woe.

Every girl in Random who passed through her class learned this ditty by heart and recited it no doubt to her children — grandchildren by now — but remained unaware of its authorship, tracing it no doubt to that no-man's-land of popular inspiration, where saws about the weather rub shoulders with hopscotch jingles, words of proverbial wisdom with "Saint Antony, you old scamp, you've found my property, just give it back to me." Our aunt, who would blush like a schoolgirl at the slightest compliment, believed no doubt that literary glory, however local, was incompatible with humility, that cardinal virtue. Fear of infringing on dogma may have had something to do with it. Association with nuns had ended by convincing her that self-satisfaction was the beginning of sin. Just as she had given up all thought of love, motherhood, and most earthly pleasures, she conscientiously compressed that part of herself in which her poetic inspiration was rooted.

Her homemade book of prayers included several versions of her Saint Christopher. In one he is a Loire ferryman at Le Pèlerin, where there actually is a ferry. But the great river is not as easily crossed as the Red Sea, and our little aunt changed her mind. To avoid sinking into the sandy bottom, the good giant would need fifty-foot stilts. And so she made him the patron saint of the dockers (a discreet regional annexation to those in the know) and went back to the old legend. Little Jesus riding on the giant's shoulders did not seem to clash with her orthodoxy. Whenever Father acquired a new car, she made him decorate the dashboard with the bronze likeness of the kindly giant, which invariably brought him good luck — hundreds of thousands of miles without a scratch. The traffic then was not what it is today, but neither were the roads. Saint Christopher is good value.

The existence of Antony of Padua is attested: born in Lisbon, joined the Franciscan order, great traveler, great preacher, numbered among the doctors of the church. How, with such credentials, did he come to be assigned to the lost-and-found department? Impenetrable are the ways of the Lord. Be that as it may, we succeeded, with his aid alone, in finding: the keys to Father's car in the linen closet, Nina's baptismal chain under the box tree in the garden, Grandmother's spectacles hanging from her neck, the prize in the Twelfth Night cake, the seven-year-old rascal who broke open the collection boxes in church, promised never to do it again, and did it again, our way when we were lost in the woods. Having to call so eminent a saint an old scamp made our little aunt uncomfortable. She took a higher view of saintly intercession. According to her lights, she addressed Saint Antony in a quatrain which, unlike the one to Saint Christopher, never went outside the family.

> Good, kind Saint Antony
> I pray on bended knee
> That you may shine your light
> And help me find my pennies bright.

This made us envision Diogenes walking the streets of Athens with his lantern, supposedly in search of an honest man but actually looking for some coins that had gone astray the night before while he was rolling dead drunk in the gutter. Consequently, we were not in the least impressed by the figure of the sovereign tramp; as far as we were concerned, Diogenes was just an old penny-pincher.

What could ever go wrong in our lives? A lighted candle on the altar ensured our success in exams; Saint Joseph watched over the family; Saint Christopher over the car and Saint Theresa over our health; Saint Victor maintained a clement microclimate over our town, while the Virgin, all-powerful in her numerous incarnations, not only guaranteed a sunny month of May, an abundant harvest, happy pregnancies, and the return of young conscripts, but also dispensed a thousand antidotes making it possible to pass unharmed through the calamities of this world. At the death of our Marie, we found, under the statues of the saints that she had secreted in every nook and cranny in the garden wall and at the back of the pious pictures in her room, dozens of folded little pieces of paper, each with a prayer, a plea. Not for her, but for the members of her little family. That J. should be immune to accidents, that business should pick up at the shop, that N. should have a successful school year, that D. should get his job and Y. his health back, that Z.'s death should be tranquil, illuminated by the certainty of the resurrection. When intercession proved unsuccessful, the saint was in disgrace, his statue was turned to the wall as a naughty child might be made to stand in the corner. The day after Father's death, Saint Joseph, a robust alabaster carpenter carrying his child on one arm, was made to face the back of his niche. This decisive failure might have been taken as a sign that the age of miracles was ended forever. Aunt Marie, however, was convinced that she alone was at fault. She couldn't forgive herself for forgetting to invoke the specialized saint who prevents clots from blocking the flow of blood between the heart and the brain. How could anyone imagine that a soul would crumple for no reason at all at the age of forty?

Aunt Marie — who, we hope, is in the holy of holies — take pity on us who have had to take our exams without your candles, confront life without your prayers, and live like disarmed, bewildered soldiers, without the strength or the example of your nephew, our father (a hundred years of indulgence).

With the coming of the first mild weather at the end of the winter months, she kept the door to her house open to admit light or the sound of the rain. In the morning she ritually strewed the crumbs from her breakfast over the threshold. In principle all birds were invited to the feast, but the robin, on watch in his pear tree, kept the sparrows and tits at bay, and they had to be satisfied with his leavings. His little red breast throbbed with indignation at the approach of an intruder. Hopping over the slab of finely honey-combed cement, he enjoyed his meal in perfect peace, sure of his strength. "My robin," she said — an unusual posses-sive for her who possessed nothing (she referred to her house, for example, as "the house in Joseph's garden").

She who treated children and domestic animals with a kind of rough tenderness (she would ring a bell in the ear of poor Pyrrhus, Rémi's spaniel, to make him stop howling whenever a siren blew) got along splendidly with the birds: no excessive displays of affection, just good-neighborly rela-tions marked by silence and respect for each other's terri-tory. After all, they were so much alike: tiny body, head tucked between shoulders in the same way, same drab plum-age, same dolls' house meals (if ever she was persuaded on the occasion of some festivity to accept a drop of something, the drop would never be more than a thimbleful), same early hours, same fluttery discretion. She told us how her robin would alight on her kitchen table, how she would go on with her work, in which he, not the least bit shy, even seemed to take an interest, his head always in motion, as though cu-rious to know the how and the why. We had to take her word

for it though, for in our presence the robin would merely dive
down to pick up his crumbs and withdraw to his pear tree
with his prey. Their little act was strictly private.

On our way across the garden, we had only to cast a
glance through the open door to surprise our aunt in her
domestic activities. Always seated at her table or desk,
absorbed — what application she devoted to the slightest
task, with the sole exception of housework, which she
considered a waste of time and scamped. Her sewing was
like her cooking. Her method of darning consisted of running a draw-thread around a hole and pulling it tight, the
result being strange wrinkles in her dresses. Her Thursdays,
when there was no school, were devoted to the parish
newsletter, which she prepared and distributed in the afternoon, house by house, always announcing herself with the
same word, "Mail" — to which she added mischievously,
"from God," which had become a kind of password, pronounced simultaneously by letter carrier and addressee.
The same at every door, with an occasional slight variation
for fear of boring her audience. Nothing obliged her to fold
each letter carefully in four and wrap it in a band inscribed
with name and address — only her pleasure in delivering
communications from heaven.

Before sitting down to table, she thrust her right hand
into an old black glove, worn only on this occasion and
serving to protect her fingers as she folded the letters from
the still-fresh printer's ink. Her rudimentary origami, performed with movements of methodical precision, suffused
the tiny kitchen, where she worked facing the wall, with a
contemplative atmosphere, as though time were granting
itself a breathing spell while the pink, green, yellow, or blue
newsletters accumulated on the oilcloth in piles of ten —
over ten, the piles collapsed.

Sometimes we were seized by a desire to help her. She moved over and the four of us set to work on three sides of the table. With one eye on her technique and the other on what we were doing, we tried to copy her movements as faithfully as possible, but try as we might we could not capture the mood of hushed transparence that fascinated us when we looked in from outside. It was like those games played in the dead of the holiday season, the suggestion of which, thrown out as a life buoy, struck us as the obvious remedy for our boredom but which, barely begun, were felt to fall far short of our expectation. If the truth be known, she had her doubts about our enthusiasm and its likely consequences; though flattered by our interest in her efforts, those of a humble ant in the universal evangelical mission, our offers of assistance did not give her unmitigated pleasure. Still, she could not refuse three young recruits permission to enlist in the legions of Christ. Actually she never refused Joseph's children anything. But, as she was only too well aware, she was letting herself in for a fine mess.

By the time we had folded some fifteen or twenty newsletters, our work showed signs of slackness. The four corners of the paper, which were supposed to come together in a single right angle, moved farther and farther apart. A little more folding and our letters began to look like fans. Our aunt sighed, examined our work, unfolded, flattened with her gloved hand, refolded, and there you are, just do as I do, it doesn't take a magician to fold a sheet of paper in four. Yes, of course, now we've got it. Full of good resolutions, we'd start in again, but before long boredom took hold. Soon the corners were again failing to coincide, and after another little while we were again turning out fans. It was the last straw when, picking up a clumsily folded newslet-

ter, we covered our eyes with it and smirked like a Carmen-
cita. That was the end of our aunt's serenity. We witnessed
the diminutive tantrum of a sparrow splashing about in a
puddle. Horrified, she tore the newsletter out of our hands
and stamped her foot while readjusting her gold-rimmed
spectacles: if we came to give her twice as much work, she'd
prefer to make out on her own. And, she added in a kind of
theatrical aside but loud enough for us to hear, she was
used to it. In this last reproach she hinted at the dreary
mystery of her existence and summed up the many renun-
ciations to which she owed her saintly reputation. We
vaguely understood: we'd think for a moment of her tiny
interior, whose only concession to ornament was a post
office calendar, of her gray, stooped shape and austere,
cramped, monotonous life — and for a moment we'd re-
pent, promising ourselves to mend our ways.

When the folding operation was complete, she would
cut bands of white paper, to be used as wrappers for the
letters, and paste the ends together. She would spread the
paste with a tiny plastic spatula, which never failed to break
under pressure. She would replace it with a match, the
unsulfured end of which she would dip into the paste. Since
she never threw anything away, these matches had a way of
sticking to her fingers and when she lit the gas she would
have to blow them out hastily.

If she had put up with us thus far, it was now that she
suffered her hardest trial — the ruination of the white paper she had been at such pains to salvage. Anxiously, she
would watch as, scissors in hand, we set out to make bor-
ders, garlands, and, inevitably, doilies. Sheets of paper four
or five times folded, cut out, notched, and grooved look so
fantastically lacy when unfolded. Proudly we displayed our
handiwork, and our poor aunt, looking at us with a

pinched smile through the artistic holes in her lovely paper, tried hard to approve.

In the last phase of the operation we managed to be almost useful. She would open a notebook containing a list of subscribers and hold it out to us. Taking turns, we would slowly read the names aloud, and she would copy them in her elegant schoolmistress's hand, with upstrokes and downstrokes, showing some irritation when we read too fast or neglected to mention "deceased" after the name of a certain party. The band that could not be used served her later as scrap paper.

This exercise had a soothing effect on us. We would joke mildly about two or three rather comical names, always the same, but reading these lists with their echo of the last roll call kept us serious in the main. Between names we heard the scraping of the pen over the paper, the woodpecker's *tic-tac* as it struck the bottom of the inkwell, the gliding of the hand over the blotting paper to dry the ink, our aunt's sighs. Her white head leaning over her work, she bade us with her eyes to continue. This copyist's labor was the substance of her *Très Riches Heures*.

Her work done, she returned what ink was left to the bottle, wiped her pen, and wrapped it in a square of cloth, lest the nib be blunted by the wood of the pen tray.

She wanted nothing to do with ballpoint pens, though Father was wildly enthusiastic about them and sang their praises wherever he went. To him they meant liberation, one more instance of progress shaking off the yoke of servitude. No more of those fountain pens that poured ink into the inside pockets of his jackets and made spots on his shirts. Traveling salesmen, those irrigators of modern life, swore by the invention. He had tried to convince Aunt Marie that ballpoint pens were the future, that her pupils would soon be using them. Hadn't the goose quill been abandoned in favor of the steel nib? One must keep up with the times. But Aunt Marie, who felt that she had done exceedingly well by her times, was deaf to his arguments, incorruptible. As she saw it, the ballpoint pen had ushered in an era of decadence; gone were upstrokes and down-strokes; next, she foresaw, the agreement of the past parti-ciple would be abandoned, not to mention the sequence of tenses, the exceptions to this rule and that rule, the circum-flex, and those dizzying irregular verbs that she taught with the help of magic formulas. ("I am beginning to perceive that the verb *apercevoir* has only one 'p.' ") The ballpoint pen was a Trojan horse as big as the Four Horsemen of the Apocalypse, a kind of terminal Babel that would swallow up the language and the world. For language partakes of the Creation, that is, of the divine. The fate of humanity is balanced on the point of a Sergeant-major brand pen.

Actually, what she dreaded most of all was that her gifts would no longer be needed. By stealth she had added five years to her statutory working life, but thanks to some sort of medal rewarding her for half a century of meritorious service the authorities had caught up with her. Their Jesuitical offer of a well-earned rest was accompanied by a little celebra-tion, the purpose of which was, no doubt, to forestall any possible return by making her say good-bye in the presence of witnesses. In attendance were the mayor, the curé, vicars, nuns with special permission to leave the convent for the occasion, missionaries in transit, notables, almost all of her former pupils — three generations, including a sprinkling of grandmothers. Those unable to attend in person had sent messages, which were read aloud. Memories by the car-load. A platform had been erected in the yard. Shaken with emotion, twisting her fingers like a little girl, Aunt Marie stood there acknowledging homages, blushing when a notable embraced her (his sharp, smacking kiss could be heard over the loudspeaker), then bravely launching into an improvisation, in which she stammered thanks, expressed her regret at leaving the home of a lifetime — but we must make way for the young, must we not? Obviously she didn't believe a word of it, convinced as she was that after her the deluge — read: ballpoint pens and slovenly grammar — and concluded her speech on a humorous note, informing all subscribers to the parish newsletter that on the coming Thursday they would again be in receipt of their little communication from heaven. There. She had managed to work it in. Meaning: You haven't buried me yet. But not a tear when she had expected floods. She was visibly sulking as she stepped down from the platform.

From then on she performed her parish duties with redoubled zeal, for which she was roundly ridiculed by Mathilde, her brother Emile's widow, who took liberties with religion that horrified our Marie. Marie got even by observing airily that the petunias in the garden of her sister-in-law, who took special pride in her flowerbeds, were thinner and not nearly as well shaped as those in the curé's garden. To which Mathilde had a ready answer: that she didn't sprinkle them with holy water. Aunt Marie shrugged her shoulders, uttered a contemptuous "Pfft" accompanied by a shower of saliva, and walked away grumbling. The old ladies had been going on like this for years, and no one paid much attention to their squabbles. They had been Siamese rivals ever since one and the same man, husband and brother, had brought them together. Their hostilities could be tempered by a tortuous tenderness. A few hours after their altercation, when Aunt Marie failed to reappear, Mathilde went to her cottage with an offer of leftover soup that she would otherwise have thrown away, and Aunt Marie demonstrated her humility by accepting it. On another occasion Mathilde, without asking leave, knitted a shawl for her rival on the pretext that Marie disgraced us all with the rags she wore over her shoulders. And always the same remarks about Marie's bigotry. A way of bringing back their girlhoods — comparative accounts of affection given and received — and in every dispute the reproach, now diluted by the passage of time, that the other was in some way responsible for the misfortune that had befallen them. Just what the petunias say to one another in the language of flowers.

Aunt Marie kept herself frantically busy with her parish work and affected to wonder who would pick up the torch when she was gone. No problem. After her death the newsletters were deposited at the baker's, and people helped themselves when buying their bread. The only losers were subscribers who lived far away and arranged to have the parish news sent them by mail, so as to learn, sometimes at the end of the world (missionaries), that at seven-thirty on the fifth of the month a Mass would be celebrated in memory of So-and-so, recalled to his maker exactly a year ago, that on the seventh the marriage of young Monsieur This to young Mademoiselle That would be celebrated, or that the dearly beloved Monsieur Something-or-other had passed away in his seventy-fifth year — thoughts, prayers, *requiescat in pace.*

After Father's death neglect took over. With barbarous indifference events pursued their lazy downhill course: the garden invaded by weeds, the path bordered by green moss, the box tree left unpruned, stagnant puddles in the yard, where no one bothered to replace the flagstones, the brick wall full of holes, objects waiting to be put away, everlasting temporary patchwork. Everything slowly and irresistibly withering away.

Some days after the funeral Julien the grave digger brought us three precious objects he had dug up in the family vault: Father's parents' two wedding rings and his mother's gold denture. With the humility of the untouchable, Julien timidly deposited his treasure on the kitchen table. He had started out as a farmhand, the lowest caste in the rural hierarchy, who in return for the sweat of his brow was lodged in the barn and given a meal for pay. For him the post of municipal grave digger was more than an unhoped-for promotion; it was a kind of knighthood. A metaphor had got him the job. He was quoted as having said at the grave side of his employer, "The dead are like seed; we put them in the ground, and then it's up to the heavens." Perhaps it is because they buried their dead that the first men, confident of resurrection, came up with the optimistic idea of putting seeds in the ground. Be that as it may, the anecdote was good for Julien's standing, giving him a reputation for the kind of "depth" needed for companionship with the dead. When his name was mentioned, people would say that in contact with nature solitude often takes on a cosmic dimension — a notion fully as plausible as the legend that a falling apple led Newton to conceive the law of gravity. When the job of municipal grave digger became vacant, the mayor and his council, impressed by this paragon of popular wisdom, had no hesitation about giving it to the unemployed farmhand-philosopher.

At first he thought more maxims were expected of him and never missed an opportunity to remark, "Stones are the bones of the earth." But failing to recapture the inspiration of his beginnings, he wisely confined himself to his trade. In view of his familiarity with the dead, he allowed himself the privilege when directing operations of talking in a loud voice, which drowned out the murmurs of visitors to the cemetery, and established his local power. Taking long steps in his green rubber boots, he stalked from grave to grave like a cat, in his muddy, oft-patched overalls, his beret well down over his eyes. In hot weather his liter of wine would be cooling in a bucket beside the one tap in the cemetery, on which he hung his jacket. He would straighten a vase overturned by the wind, pull up a blade of grass, rake the sand covering a grave, straighten a crucifix, delicately arrange a bunch of flowers with his horny hands, gnarled from constantly gripping the spade. Bonaparte of an army of shades, he would have liked to tweak the ears of his dead, had he not been afraid of their coming off in his hands.

His day of glory was All Saints' Day, when he sold potted chrysanthemums on his own account. He displayed his wares on a table consisting of three boards supported by two trestles at the entrance to the graveyard. With the help of his son, Yvon, who, strictly speaking, was not his, he played the businessman. As soon as he had three customers, he hurried from one to the other like a valet in an Italian comedy, always bent double, constantly pushing up his beret with his thumb with the air of a man too busy to catch his breath. This was also a way of clearing his head, of taking time to think before closing a deal, as he wasn't very good at figures. To make it easier for himself, he would round out his prices to the nearest zero, with the result that, depending on the year, it was more profitable to buy three-bloom or four-bloom plants. From the back pocket of his trousers, whose crotch hung down to his knees, he extracted a thick leather wallet and slipped bank notes into it with the assurance of a horse dealer. Yvon contented himself with a cardboard imitation, an empty Chantenay sugar box, folded and refolded so as to form two compartments, one for bank notes, the other for coins. Mathilde, for whom he gardened a few hours a week, had given him one of her son Rémi's old wallets freshly mended and polished, but the next time he came he again brought out his contraption, which he presented as a model of ingenuity and the proof of an able mind. Indeed, he was closer to *Homo habilis* than *Homo sapiens*; no one knew whether he was his uncle's or his grandfather's son, but this pharaonic heritage had undoubtedly left its traces. His adoptive father employed him to deliver the pots of chrysanthemums that were not sold at the Random cemetery. Yvon carried them in a basket attached somehow or other to his baggage carrier, mounted his bicycle, turned his cap front to back, and sped through the town shouting, "Atta boy, Bobet!"

Everybody made fun of him. Even when he was a child, his schoolmates picked on him. Their great sport had been to corner him at the foot of the Tour d'Enfer, a ramshackle vestige of a medieval tower, and throw stones at him. In school he enjoyed a kind of amnesty thanks to the presence of the teacher, who, however, regularly cited him as an example not to follow. Recess as a rule went off fairly well,

except on rainy days, when the favorite sport was splashing
him with puddle water. His worst torment began with the
mad five o'clock exodus. He would take his position at the
foot of the tower and wait for the stones to fall, holding his
schoolbag over his face like a shield. The stones rained
down, striking his pathetic shield with a dull thud. After
dodging and parrying for a while, he would summon up the
courage to confront his assailants and fight back with in-
sults. His favorite insult was a kind of onomatopoeia in
patois that became his tormentors' nickname for him when
they were really out to get him. Sometimes a stone hit him
in the shin and he could be seen dancing like an Indian. Or
else he would collapse, howling and yelping, which instead
of arousing the sympathy of his enemies sent them into
gales of laughter. There was no one to deflect the thunder-
bolts from this ideal lightning rod.

With so perfect a victim to work on, misfortune was not
chary of its inexhaustible resources. At the age of fifteen he
began to see lizards climbing up the wall, soon accompanied by the whole fantastic bestiary of delirium tremens,
not to mention the real rats under his bed. At Julien's death
not a single clean sheet could be found in the house with its
beaten earth floor. Recognized as Julien's heir, Yvon swag-
gered a little. The women who passed him in the street
thought him vicious because he looked at them in a way
they described as sneaky but was mostly lecherous. They all
avoided poor Yvon. He was found dead in a ditch, suffering
from advanced cirrhosis, lying beside his bicycle — his
faithful life companion — hit no doubt by a car, which had
finished the job begun by his schoolmates. The police were
quick to close the affair, and no one came forward to
protest. Everyone agreed that nothing better could have

happened to him. Yvon died at the age of twenty-nine, more alone than a dog — his life in a nutshell.

Yvon was there too when Julien brought Aline's gold denture and the two wedding rings. Standing in the kitchen door after depositing their treasures on the table and taking a step backward, they were waiting for a little something more than thanks. Mother slipped each of them a coin. A fairly sizable one for Julien, and for Yvon — as she herself put it — something to buy candy with. When they showed no sign of wanting to move, she realized that she had forgotten the main thing. She apologized, but her thoughts were elsewhere, and her eyes, spent with grief and barely holding back the tears, hesitated. Julien, embarrassed, mumbled something that was supposed to be a formula of condolence, but gave up after finding himself out of his depth, and made a vague gesture of wanting to leave. Mother insisted. Surely he would accept a glass of wine. He went through the motions of declining, he didn't want to impose . . . but then, after all, he didn't say no. And for his little boy? Oh, the same, he was used to it, he wasn't afraid of a glass of wine. And by his way of acquiescing, Yvon, standing there with a greasy strand of hair stuck to his forehead, made it clear enough that he was not afraid. Mother, who was, suggested that he might prefer the mild syrup the children drank. Yvon blushed, looked at the carpet, and said nothing. No, no, no complications, same as his father — said his father.

In the end there were no complications; it was mint syrup for all. Mother remembered too late that she had no wine in the house, we were a family of water drinkers and bought wine only on special occasions, when guests were expected.

When mother poured water into the syrup, Julien stopped her as if she were drowning his pastis. He had never before tasted anything of the kind, and only the young widow's grief stopped him from declining. He tasted it, smacked his lips, and declared that it wasn't bad. A short-lived conversion — he, too, was carried off by liver trouble.

Glass in midair and hand on hip, Yvon adopted his father's pose, standing firmly planted in his rubber boots, whose aroma gradually invaded the room. To fill in the silence, Mother congratulated the grave digger on his honesty. Others in his position might not have been as scrupulous.

That was one way of looking at it. Another might have been to imagine Julien concealing his misdeed by secretly melting down his gold in his wretched hovel and selling his ingot to the local jeweler — Rémi, whose shop was next door to our house. Obviously it was simpler for the philosophical gardener to content himself with a tip and a glass of wine.

His find, when he had left, was put on the sideboard along with numerous objects and papers waiting to be sorted and put away. The resulting mountain collapsed whenever we tried to extract something from it. One component was a chipped ceramic fruit bowl, a sumptuous tachist, resolutely modern affair. Years later, the few nuts in this bowl, the only fruit it had ever contained, put there as decorative accessories on the day of its enthronement in the middle of the sideboard, were exhumed when John, who was paying us a visit, confided that he liked to wind up his meals with a handful of dried fruit. Someone remembered the nuts, having probably caught a glimpse of them at the time of the last landslide. It took considerable excavation to reach them, but sure enough, there they were, still at the bottom of the bowl, white, clean and bleached, a victory over time. Our rejoicing was short-lived. The inside was dust, and the few almonds that could be saved were so shriveled and dry that we felt like grave robbers, eating the funeral repast provided to sustain the deceased on his long journey.

If we needed a screw, a nut, a tube of paste, a razor blade, a watch spring, a marble, a pin, a pencil, a paper clip, a coin with a hole in it (for use as a washer), or the tiny watchmaker's screwdriver that we used to tighten the hinges of our glasses, we had only to plunge into the biotope between the china cupboard and the top of the sideboard and locate the glass hors d'oeuvres dish that had served as a bath for the little white garnet-billed mandarin birds which, we never found out why, had one after another been found dead in their cage. It was in this butter dish— swimming pool that the wedding rings were deposited on the supposition that they might come in handy someday, and there, too, that the denture ended up. Its career as a prosthesis was undoubtedly at an end, but, just as it has become fashionable to convert a bugle into a bedside lamp or an oxen yoke into a chandelier, one could always hope for some prodigy of recycling.

At first we were horrified at the thought of such a monstrosity in the mouth of a human being. It seemed more like an instrument of torture, a means of extracting confessions. The whole thing — teeth, palate, gums — was gold. It was heavy, ungainly, and cumbersome. If found in an archaeological dig, it might have been attributed to Scythian goldsmiths or the surgeons of the Eighteenth Dynasty. But what might, in the mouth of Queen Hatshepsut, have elicited wonderment had us worrying about the comfort and well-being of our gold-mouthed grandmother.

Grandmother Aline was definitely not the complaining

sort. Her life had been marked by a series of tragedies, or rather by a repetition of the same tragedy, all her children stillborn up to the late and miraculous Joseph, our father, who must have inherited a sense of the fragility of existence, since in spite of his imposing stature, he died at the age of forty.

Aline's sufferings had left her with a latent sadness that struck all who knew her, a sadness further accentuated by the softness of her voice. Ah, that voice — all who heard it agreed — no sooner had she opened her golden mouth than one forgot the massive, ungainly body that the poor woman moved around the shop with the deliberate lightness of those, including some of the smallest and lightest, who are afraid of taking up too much room.

The denture was in her image. Overflowing the butter dish–swimming pool, it spoke for her. Now the nuts and bolts and erasers were crowded. At the least disturbance of the sideboard we'd find them spread out on the gray kitchen linoleum, featherless chicks ruthlessly ejected from the nest by the parasitical cuckoo. Something had to be done. We lifted up the corner of the tabletop and inserted the heavy denture as a support. With its weight it prevented cave-ins at the base.

We stopped paying attention to it. It took a visitor's look of alarm to remind us of its incongruity. Later on, quite naturally, it came to be used as a paperweight. A letter, an urgent bill would be displayed in plain sight under the mighty golden jaw. We ate our meals beside it without being the least bit bothered or impressed.

The whole place was going to the dogs. Never in his life-time would our hyperactive father have allowed the gates to be dismantled. His vigilance did not allow a crack to form, a painted surface to flake, a roof to leak, or a pipe to drip. Give him Venice and he'd have saved the Serenissima from the waters. He'd have cemented façades, coated woodwork with Formica, drained the canals, and put the gondolas on rails, but Venice would have been saved. For our garden he had a project worthy of the Grand Siècle, with rocks, waterfalls, and flowery arbors. Aunt Marie was beginning to worry about the place he was setting aside for his statues. His folly is attested by a pencil sketch and a number of granite blocks brought from the interior of Brit-tany in the trunk of his car. Piled up against the back wall of the garden, they soon disappeared in the tall grass.

These Herculean labors overshadowed the more delicate aspect of his restoration work, his repairing of dolls, his daughters', it goes without saying, but also — what with his growing reputation — those of all the little girls of the vicinity, who would hopefully bring him their one-eyed or one-armed babies. He put the detached parts back in place. For the missing ones he collected, among the boxes of nails in his workshop, parts recovered from dolls that had been beyond repair: eyes, heads, arms, legs — like a display of ex-votos. Some of the dolls, when called for, had eyes of different colors and one leg shorter or pinker than the other, but the little girls didn't seem to know the difference.

Built by our father's father, the garage at the far end of the garden was shut off from the street by a metal door, which at the time was no doubt thought to be innovative. The celebrity of the Eiffel Tower and the glory of the Wendels must have had something to do with Pierre's choice. Fearing to miss the modernist train, he had let himself be convinced that iron would be more resistant, that this armor would offer his household the best protection against the ravages of time.

For lack of maintenance — it should have been scraped and repainted every three years — rust easily overcame its resistance. Little ochre atolls appeared around the rivets, expanding little by little into islands and continents which like a coral-colored sea gangrened the green planisphere of the door. Toward the end, only a few trails of residual paint recalled its Pompeiian past. The pressure of a finger sufficed to make a peephole in the sheet metal. Oxidized and corroded, it peeled like the bark of a plane tree. Just before we replaced it, the door became so dangerous that we were ordered to keep away from it. Apart from the possibility of being infected with tetanus by an iron splinter, we were always in danger of being crushed by the heavy panels or stabbed by a loose strip of metal. Bulky parcels were now delivered through Rémi's adjoining garden, to the delight of the swallows that nested under the eaves of the garage and, now that there was no one to interfere with them, whirled round and round, squeaking softly, in the abandoned storeroom.

This door had always been hard to manage. It folded like a screen, and to close it, it was better to be two than one, or if that couldn't be managed, to be big and strong like Father. The operation consisted of hugging the panels to your body and at the same time inserting the lugs attached to them into the grooves in the floor and roof. But your arm got tired holding these enormous metal panels, the blood drained from your upraised arm, and many a time, while you were aiming for the grooves in the enormous lintel beam, a flake of rust would fall into your eye. When that happened, you dropped everything to rub your eye and, overcome by impotent rage, despaired of ever succeeding. This operation, natural in the days when Father attended to it with the monumental strength characteristic of fathers, made it clear to us after his death that our road would henceforth be beset with perils, to combat which one would need the hard soul of an icebreaker, which we, capable only of sniveling like mournful Robinson Crusoes washed up on an island of darkness, did not have.

The wooden door that closed the garage on the garden side seems to have rotted slowly away like the hull of a ship run aground on a beach green with seaweed — owing no doubt to the combined effects of the Atlantic rains and the repeated blows of the soccer balls that shook the old planks. First came creaking sounds, then small fissures appeared, and then one day the ball passed through the door amid a shower of splinters, traversed the garage, and thudded against the metal wall. With the passing years the boards hung more and more loosely from the iron fittings, until at length they broke loose and fell into the grass, where they lay like a negligent throw of jackstraws.

Some years after the war a penniless boy of twenty, a painter, turned up in our town. He seemed so forlorn that Father supplied him with his garage to paint in, brushes to paint with, and work to live on. When he became engaged, the young man painted the first name of his betrothed in golden letters on the inside of the door, which he used as a giant palette on which to try out his colors. Later, perhaps as a result of a quarrel, he covered the name with a discreet black rectangle. After a while we forgot it. But later on, when the rain had many times washed those old boards, it reappeared, exhumed like a miniature Troy of love.

Aunt Marie wouldn't have tolerated this neglect, this deterioration of our heritage. She would have combated the ravages of time with the same energy she showed when mopping up the gallons of water a burst pipe had disgorged into her kitchen. All night she had fought bravely like Monsieur Séguin's goat, alone with her rags, her feet in the water, bailing, wringing, emptying bucket after bucket, as usual unwilling to disturb anyone, asking help only of the person whose name in her card file was placed under "water damage." The next day, exhausted, she came over and admitted that she would probably need Joseph, as she feared that her rag poultice wouldn't hold out for long. Called in to judge the extent of the disaster, Joseph expressed his admiration for her persistence and ingenuity and Aunt Marie was overjoyed at his praise. At other times, however (and this could lead her to sulk for hours), he made fun of her propensity for keeping everything — when he found some article that he had thrown away in the attic of her little house, or when she took it into her head to glue together the thousand pieces of a statue of Saint Anne that had fallen mysteriously from its pedestal (a prayer not granted? divine wrath?), a three-dimensional puzzle that kept her busy for many evenings with unimpressive results: a poor, scarred Saint Anne, not fully recovered from her operation, oozing paste from her wounds and cutting a pathetic figure beside her son-in-law, the alabaster carpenter. But you don't cast off a replica of the mother of the Mother of God, the woman whom Jesus called Grandmother, like a handful of dust.

Aunt Marie would have done everything in her power to oppose the pauperization of the garden. She would have fought with tubes of paste, adhesive tape, and appeals to heaven. She would have felt in duty bound to carry on the work of her departed nephew. She would have done it in memory of him.

As it turned out, she was the first to give in. She made it past New Year's Day, as though determined to reach this last milestone, after which she would rest awhile. That threshold passed, at two o'clock in the morning she was reported missing.

It was almost twelve noon, and she had still given no sign of life. It wasn't like her. Attached as she was to her independence, she was too much afraid of being alone to spend the whole morning cloistered in her little house; she was constantly going on some errand. She could get out of the garden in two different ways, through our house or Rémi's. Then she had only to cross the street to reach the church, where since her retirement she had undertaken a thorough reorganization in a Cluniac spirit. But she was also determined to show us that she had other activities. Whenever she appeared in our hallway she announced her reason for going out. She would thrust her wrinkled, skinny neck through the kitchen door and, in too much of a hurry to stop, announce in her faint fluttery voice, "I'm going out for butter" or "Monsier le curé has sent for me" or "If anyone wants me I'll be at the So-and-sos'." As often as not, the kitchen would still be empty. From upstairs we would hear her communicate her mission to the breakfast dishes awaiting us on the table. Content with that, she would put her neck back on her shoulders, and forward, O Lord, for thine is the kingdom and the power and the glory.

And so on from morning to night, when before going to bed she still had to accomplish what might be termed her motionless stations of the Cross. Kneeling on a prie-dieu of black turned wood, arms apart, palms turned heavenward as though awaiting stigmatization by heavenly laser rays, she murmured innumerable rosaries one after another. The cushion of the prie-dieu shows the stigmata of her long prayer sessions. The fabric has lost its color and texture and the stuffing feels like sackcloth under your knees. The arm-rest is in better shape, the green velvet is just a bit worn in the spot where she rests her prayer book. For she does not lean on it. She does not pray with her face in her hands as in church, where she spreads her arms and needs three chairs if she is not to slap her neighbor in the face. In the privacy of her home that would be a sign of slovenly abandon, unworthy of Him who suffered so much to obtain a remission of sins for her and for the multitude — mostly the multitude, for Aunt Marie's sins could hardly have been worth Jesus' hanging himself on the Cross.

She inclines her head to one side as when eating ceremoniously or posing for her picture — in all her photographs, her neck, too frail to hold her head upright, is out of alignment and she seems to be looking for something behind the photographer, as though he were blocking the way between her and something essential, as though in the night of her bedchamber-chapel she were trying to pierce a blanket of darkness to capture a ray of the divine light.

She still got up early, though nothing obliged her to, except the first of the three low Masses she imposed on herself. Fifty laborious years had rendered her incapable of staying in bed. The force of habit. That gave her a long day to fill. She spent her time incessantly shuttling back and forth, creating an impression of bustling activity, though we all knew that the explanations she offered were largely palliatives for the boredom she had discovered late in life.

Not wanting to make a nuisance of herself, or perhaps to avoid offending against what she imagined to be sensibilities but was only a kind of impatience, she never passed through the same house on her way back from an errand.

And it was at Rémi, bending over his worktable with his
watchmaker's magnifying glass in his eye, that she waved
her slab of butter in guise of evidence: "I've bought my
butter" (and Rémi realizes that he is expected to know that
she went out for butter), or "Monsieur le curé was out"
(and, as she doesn't want it thought that he has stood her
up, she hastens to add that Anastasie, his maid, was expect-
ing her with an apology from Monsieur le curé, who had
been called in haste to visit Madame So-and-so, most probably, alas, to administer extreme unction. And then Rémi,
who is extremely well informed about the local life that he
observes through the white Dacron curtains of his shop
window, makes the mistake of raising his head, taking the
magnifying glass out of his eye, and asking in a tone of
concern, "Madame who?" Which is just what he should
not have done, for Aunt Marie, having hooked her fish, will
be in no hurry to let him go: Madame So-and-so, of such-
and-such a village, on the road to, wife of, daughter of, but
the explanation reaches so far back — at least three generations, with births, deaths, jobs, causes of death — the ge-
nealogy becomes so elaborately ramified that it will take an
exasperated Rémi half an hour to find out that the dying
woman is the great-grandmother who is pushing a hundred; and mentally cursing Madame So-and-so, Aunt
Marie, and all those who are conspiring to waste his time,
he delivers one of his peremptory judgments: "Madame So-
and-so didn't set the world on fire" — which, after all, is no
disgrace — and gets back to work.

In the end all these comings and goings created confusion in her mind. Having announced butter she would go to
see Monsieur le curé, then on her return would slap her
forehead like the heroine of a tragedy and exclaim, "Oh, I
forgot my butter," bury her head between her shoulders,

and go out again. Her diminutive silhouette would be seen hurrying down the street, a pitter-pattering mouse for whom everyone had a friendly word. Once we distinctly heard her announce that she was going to the Magnificat and saw her rush to the privy in the yard, in memory of which, we relieved ourselves at the Magnificat for many years to come. We astonished more than one of our acquaintances with these sudden accesses of piety that ended upstairs with the sound of a tumultuously flushing toilet. But it was obvious that she was getting ready to go out of her mind. The episode of December 26 only accelerated the process and brought on new symptoms.

She spent the five days between Father's death and New Year's in a state of trance, punctuated by moments of utter dejection. We would surprise her in a chair, her head bowed like her Jesus, virtually hunchbacked, her hands clasped in the lap of her shapeless black skirt, her toes barely grazing the floor, seemingly absent, as though sudden realization of what had happened had created a fissure in the field of her thoughts. She had tried to think it through, but her mind rebelled against this death, refused to assimilate the unthinkable. The shock cut her off from the world of the living. And then on a sudden impulse she would resume her secret activities with redoubled energy. She assured us that she was attending to everything, seeing Monsieur le curé about the words and music and flowers for the funeral, and Julien about the cemetery. We could mourn in peace, she would take care of everything else. She came and went like an automaton, and then the spring would run down and she would collapse in a daze, the rims of her eyes reddened by grief and the sleepless nights during which she cried out to the Lord, proposing the oldest bargain in the world, an exchange of herself for her nephew. She felt that there had been a mistake, the blow had missed its mark, she had been the target, they should come back and get her, correct the error, there was nothing shameful about admitting a mistake. That at least is what she kept saying, but the big body in the bedroom upstairs, which Mother watched over for sixty hours without interruption, remained as rigid as ever, and toward the end gave off a dubious smell, which at first we attributed to a change in the weather. When the winds veer to the west, they pick up the gaseous emanations of the chemical plants on the banks of the Loire above Saint-Nazaire, the ammonia, sulfur, and SO_2, which vein the sky over the estuary with green and amber and are confidently interpreted as a sign of rain. But the bedroom window was closed and weatherstripped against the winter cold. And, when tested, the outside air was crystal fresh. What we smelled was life moving out. Between errands Aunt Marie went up to see how her bargain was making out, whether Father was sitting up in bed, waiting for her to come and take his place. But her illusions were gone. Something had snapped. All her life she had negotiated with the saints — taking advantage of their human side, their susceptibility to compliments, tokens of esteem, bargaining. If she played her cards right, they would refuse her nothing. But now, the order to retreat came from too high up — from the incorruptible, inaccessible. Treading softly, she went to one of the chairs placed around the bed for the wake, sat down ever so cautiously on the edge, and shut her eyes. Holding her beads between her fingers, she muttered a thousand rosaries, an obstinate, spluttering, atmospheric murmur. We could see that it got on Mother's nerves, she would have liked to tell Aunt Marie to take her prayers somewhere else, where the effect would have been the same. Her poor tired eyes begged to be left alone with the man of her life — one last time, one last favor. Moved at the sight of her ravaged features, we all pleaded with her to lie down for a little while, but time and again she refused, determined to stay with her loved one to the end, all the more so when in view of the smell it came to be rumored that it would soon be time to put Father in his coffin and he would vanish forever beneath its lid.

Rémi was the first to be alarmed. He watched through his curtains for Monsieur le curé Bideau and called out to him as he was going into the church. The priest assured him that he had not seen Aunt Marie all morning. According to Rémi, "That imbecile Bideau" saw nothing unusual about this, "even though she was always tangled up in his skirts." Rémi was the official organist. With his anticlerical utterances he compensated himself for his unpaid services to the parish — a hard week's work, three Masses, plus Vespers on Sunday and the seven o'clock service on weekday mornings, not to mention weddings and funerals. He had composed a wedding march that was famous and very much in demand, though to his chagrin some young couples preferred "the pompous one" as he put it, by Mendelssohn. When he was asked to supply the music for a service that was not covered by his contract, it only took a bit of pleading, he could never bring himself to refuse. He could kick himself. The next time, he declared, Bideau and his acolytes would leave his shop on a stretcher, but the next time it was always "Thank you, Monsieur Rémi, we knew we could count on you."

Aunt Marie's absence worried him. He wanted to mention it to Mother, but we didn't know how to approach her. We spoke to her, as one speaks to deaf-mutes, by addressing the person next to her. People would ask us how is your mother when Mother was right there, in exile, far away. It took her years to get back into the world of the living.

Backed up by his mother, Rémi decided to take action.

As usual, we were all in the kitchen, the only room that was kept really warm in the winter. In addition to eating our meals there, we played, roughhoused, studied — or, most of the time, did nothing there. The look of compassion on Mathilde's face when she saw all four of us bowed over our brand-new grief brought it home to us that our misfortune was even worse than we had imagined. Rémi apologized for breaking in on us, quickly asked how we were getting on, glossed over our answers, and came to the reason for his visit: Had we seen Aunt Marie that morning? Yes, it's true, she hadn't been by. Didn't her absence worry us? Yes, but what was the good of worrying? And anyway, our aunt was in the habit of playing hide-and-seek and reappearing just as we were beginning to worry. Even so, Rémi wanted to be on the safe side, and since we were making no move, he suggested an expedition across the garden to the cottage half hidden by the box tree. We started along the path between the rows of rosebushes, whose bare branches interlaced over the arbor. Rémi in the lead with his rolling gait, followed by Mathilde and Mother both in black, and soon joined by Pyrrhus, Rémi's crazy spaniel, who had jumped the gate — all of four feet high — between the two gardens. Apparently fearing some danger, Rémi asked the children to stay behind. At the cottage he tried to look in through the window, but the curtains were drawn, which convinced him that Aunt Marie was at home. He then advised us to go back home and, when we failed to move because Mother hadn't said anything, told us to keep our distance. The door refused to open. He would have to break a pane on a level with the window catch. Mathilde picked up a stone and handed it to Rémi, but, always the meticulous craftsman, he shook his head and sent her to fetch a diamond from the upper left-hand drawer of his work-

bench. The menial tasks were for Mathilde. Rémi got rid
of the stone by throwing it as far as he could. Pyrrhus,
who seldom understood what was expected of him, ran
after it hell for leather and brought it back in his mouth.
Apparently it wasn't playtime, for Rémi rewarded him with
a smack on the nose.

When Mathilde, aged seventy, returned breathless from
her errand, Rémi observed that it was none too soon, and
she countered by pointing out that the diamond had not
been in the upper left-hand drawer, whereupon Rémi
wanted to know who hadn't put it back where it belonged,
and wondered which of the three possible suspects — his
mother, himself, and his dog — could have been the culprit.
Aunt Marie, lying there with the sheet pulled up to her chin,
contemplated the heavens from behind her closed eyelids:
"I am ready, O Lord, whenever you wish. May a legion of
angels waft me up to you, the Most High. But what do I
hear? That scratching on the glass, followed by a brittle
snap? Is it already your messengers? Since when have those
blasphemous pillagers of souls started breaking into people's houses?" Rémi, who had cut himself putting his hand
in to turn the window catch, swore under his breath. Having won our admiration by opening the window, he sat
down on the sill, pivoted on his behind, picked up his bad
leg in both hands, and moved it through the window frame.
Once inside, he got tangled up in the curtains. When he
parted them, the light took advantage of the opening to fall
on the bed. He thought he was seeing things. There was
Mathilde, her ear pressed against Aunt Marie's miniature
chest, listening in the Indian manner for a last trace of
breath.

"How did you get in?"

"Hush!" says Mathilde.

"Is she dead?"

"Through the door," says Mathilde — her deferred answer implying that Marie's heart is still beating. Facing due west (the setting sun lit Marie's solitary and frugal evening meal), the wooden door warped by the winter rains needed only a shove to spring open. Marie had her way of bracing herself against it. We always expected to hear her bones crack. But thanks to long practice, she brought pressure to bear in the right place and took considerable pride in her talent. Actually, she never locked her door except on stormy nights when the sky breaks into a thousand pieces over the Atlantic. On such nights neither prayer nor pleas for the intercession of the Virgin of the Seas dissipated her fears, and then she would turn her key in the lock.

Her eyes closed, without her gold-plated spectacles, her white hair crushed by a hairnet, she seemed different that day, a stranger as it were, as though a substitution had been effected during the night, as though our little aunt, who could not die (how could she die at her ageless age with such powerful protectors?), had been replaced during her dormition by a vulgar look-alike mortal. This was not the aunt we knew, the vivacious, busy woman with the mischievous eyes and the unguarded tongue. What did our Marie have in common with this silent immobility, this ivory pallor — she whose hurrying through the west wind brought hectic blotches to her cheeks.

Pyrrhus, who like his master had entered through the window, jumped up on the bed, making Aunt Marie bounce on the springs. For a moment we thought she had woken up and was surprised at seeing all these people around her. But she fell back with her head across the pillow. Her hairnet slipped down over her eyes, and

Mathilde, ever so carefully, adjusted it. Rémi raised his hand and scolded under his breath, "Pyrrhus!" The big tawny dog fell heavily on the bedside rug. He didn't understand. He had wanted as usual to gratify Aunt Marie with one of his exuberant displays of tenderness that left her bewildered and her specs askew.

We took Aunt Marie to the nearest district hospital. Rémi blamed the coal stove. He claimed to have noticed an odd smell on entering the cottage, but what with Aunt Marie's way of cooking, there were always strange, unidentifiable smells in the air. The moment Dr. Maubrilland arrived he was asked to sniff. Never before would we have dared suggest so prosaic an explanation to him, but Father's death had punctured the legendary reliability of his diagnoses. Oh, that assurance, the certainty with which he had pronounced his verdicts — from now on he would have to take a humbler tone with us, for we were still in possession of Father's diary with its record of postmortem appointments for massage, recommended by the doctor as treatment for the unbearable pain in his back. And so, since we could no longer put blind trust in the doctor's judgment, all seven of us proceeded to sniff the air in the hope of detecting a noxious emanation which, we felt sure, was making us a little dizzy, and to lift the lid of the stove to make sure. The results were hardly conclusive (as it happens, carbon dioxide is odorless). And indeed, such an exit à la Zola — who is on the Index — didn't seem at all right for our little aunt.

When she opened her eyes, the hospital judged her cured and sent her back to us.

When we wake from the dead, we shall be like awkward schoolboys with brand-new bodies. We gained this knowledge from Aunt Marie, from her unusual posture as she awaited us in the upstairs room on the street side, where Mother had installed her on her return from the hospital — leaning one hand on the wooden bedstead like a world-weary Talleyrand, seeming not so much to grip it as to establish a pose, a new curve in which to inscribe her arched back, her frail limbs, and her head, as though embarrassed at having played us this low trick, almost apologizing for her sham exit, looking at us with the terrifying detachment of those who have passed beyond the confines of the sensory world. The impression we had had on finding her unconscious was confirmed: this wasn't our aunt. It was as if a part of her, the part that identified her in our eyes, had been mutilated, effaced by her stay on the fringe of darkness — while the presence of this pseudo-aunt, this silhouette shorn of its identifying marks, left us without, yes, without consciousness.

What does John say about the reappearance of Jesus on that hallucinated morning that is a stumbling block to many? Early, when it was yet dark, Mary Magdalene went to the sepulchre and found it empty — Mary Magdalene, the woman whose love was boundless, who anointed the feet of the sublime walker with costly ointment and wiped them with her hair. She asked the man whom she mistook for the gardener where the body of the crucified one had been laid, for she wished to take him away, to assure him beyond the grave that her love was everlasting. Mary Mag-

dalene did not complain of having been deceived about the
Resurrection, she did not play the part of one offended,
did not comfort herself with the hope of an amnesty; she
was not ashamed that her credulity had been abused, she
scoffed at the fear of public opinion that paralyzed the
apostles. This revelation of love was enough for her, it
would keep her to the end of her days. And He, who
understood, addressed her for the first time no doubt with
an affectionate diminutive: "Mariam," he says simply, and
she, turning, says, "Rabbi," which in Hebrew signifies "my
master" and may be taken to mean "my man, my all, my
loving care," for he is the only man capable of standing up
to this flux of love, capable of stanching it, as none of the
men who flocked to her bed had been. But now entrust this
scenario to a film director and see what he does with it
(Father, forgive them, for they know not what they do). He
would send them rushing frantically into each other's arms,
he would instruct them to embrace passionately in their joy
at being reunited, and neither Jesus nor Mary Magdalene
nor the director would have understood the essence of the
Resurrection. "Touch me not," said the Master. To us
Mother said, "Kiss your aunt."

We didn't dare — we had no desire to thrust our hands
into her lungs impaired by the smoke from her stove, no
desire to believe in this ghost. And anyway, Aunt Marie had
never known how to kiss: she touched her dry cheek to the
cheek we held out to her in a quick electrostatic contact and
smacked her lips in the void — that passed for a demonstra-
tion of affection. She never threw her arms around you or
fondled you, she never pressed you to her bosom, not even
her Jesus whom she embraced at arm's length, not even
babies, for whom she assumed the stance of andirons holding a log. A photograph taken in the courtyard shows her

holding Nina, aged two months, on a level with her face, very much as a triumphant athlete might hold his trophy. Nina is turned toward the photographer — Father, no doubt — while Aunt Marie with her biblical modesty is hiding behind the child.

Her deficient sensuality did not make for effusiveness. Each in turn, we stepped up to her. She let go of the bedstead and rested her hands on our shoulders. For her this form of embrace — the best she could manage — was unprecedented. We felt that she had wanted to mark the event, her unlikely return to the land of the living, a needlessly emphatic gesture. She had always been tiny, but her stay in the hospital had shrunk her a little more, as though she had started withdrawing into herself.

Embraces of this kind are a problem for people who wear glasses. They have to give the face a wide berth, keep far enough away to avoid collision with the rims. Her fear of disaster and distaste for contact with flesh always led our little aunt to attempt a wider flanking movement than necessary, with the result that we ended by kissing the gold button in her earlobe. This ornament should not be interpreted as coquetry on her part: in those days it was customary to pierce the ears of little girls, who were consulted no more than the victims of excision. These gold buttons, implanted some months after birth, often at the cost of copious bleeding, stayed with them until death, a ritual providing a kinship between our most Christian aunt and certain barbarian princesses: it was with this sensation of cold metal on our lips ("Lord," said Saint Thomas, "they forgot a nail in your wound") that we took leave of her.

Later on she went out of her mind. At first it didn't worry us very much. In view of her age and the seismic shock we had suffered it didn't seem too extraordinary that

she should ask where Joseph was. Even with a corpse under
your nose it is hard for death to sink in. I remember how
one evening, when I was watching television at Rémi's, I
suddenly jumped up to tell Father about a soccer score that
would have interested him. My hand was already on the
doorknob when it all came back to me. We told Aunt Marie
that Father was on the road, that his business was taking
him farther and farther away, but that he would be back
soon. She pretended to accept our explanations, but after
thinking it over awhile she started in again. She could see
that something was wrong.

It was agreed that she would move to Rémi's as soon as a
room could be gotten ready for her. She couldn't possibly
have gone back to her cottage with its awful stove, and
Mother hadn't the strength to keep her. To make her feel at
home we moved her most precious belongings: her crucifix,
her pictures from Lourdes and Lisieux, her card file that she
had just brought up to date, plus a few knickknacks and a
collection of pious medals to slip into the cupboards and
under her pillow. She insisted from the first that the crucifix
wasn't hers, that hers had been stolen and she would complain about it to Joseph on his return. Rémi tried to dis-
prove her contention, but gave up in the face of her
obstinacy. Mathilde sent him back to his workbench and
calmly took over. The crucifix, she agreed, had been stolen,
but God help the thief, Joseph would be sure to catch him
when he got back. That, said Aunt Marie, was what she had
been saying all along, she wasn't crazy, and in the meantime
she didn't want this one. Mathilde, who affected to believe
that her sister-in-law was unable to sleep in the same room
with a half-naked stranger, slipped the crucifix into the
drawer of the dressing table.

Pyrrhus, who was glad to have his old friend back, spent

his days in her room stretched out on the bed. From time to time he would go downstairs and pay a short visit to Rémi in the shop, get a friendly pat on the head and another one, less certain, from Mathilde. Then, having made sure that everything was all right, he would return to his post upstairs. He was obviously so imbued with his role, so conscious of his responsibility, that to allay any possible worry it sufficed to say, "Pyrrhus is with her."

She kept asking for Joseph, and the answer was always the same. On the road, there had been some slipup, but he wouldn't be long. Boredom might almost have made us spill the beans. Little by little the extent of the misunderstanding was revealed — by her shifts, her wanderings away from the realm of the absurd, which we conceded to her. For instance: Joseph was wounded. He needed her help, she must go to him, we must take her to Tours — and then something about Belgium. Tours, all right — the Loire Valley, Orléans, Beaugency were like an extension of the estuary — but where did Belgium come in? Actually, Father had tried his luck in Brussels in the days when he was trying to sell educational pictures to Catholic schools (with so little success that we still have an enormous stock of them in the garden shed, the whole Old Testament in thirty color plates), but during the last few years he had concentrated on pottery and remained within the confines of Brittany. We were aware of Aunt Marie's mania for framing her stories in vast retrospective panoramas, as though to her mind the surest way of finding Father was to work backward from the present, to reverse the flow of time. We recognized that there was a certain skill in her way of mixing things up and that her mind dwelled in a fourth, space-time dimension where it was impossible to follow her. She insisted that Joseph was wounded. Haunted by

visions, she seemed to have received a call from Father
through some mediumistic channel: he'd had an accident,
he was lying helpless by the roadside, imprisoned in the
crushed carcass of his car. We comforted ourselves with the
thought that where he was, nothing more could happen
to him.

It was Mathilde who disentangled the skein of her old
accomplice's thoughts. One by one she extracted the
threads and restored the fabric of her memory. The whole
story was there. Marie had lost her wits the better to re-
cover them. The confusion had its source not in her but in
us, in our reading of her visions. The core of the matter was
that, immersed in our grief, we assumed that Father was the
only Joseph to have died since the official inception of the
universe, that is, the time to which our memories extended.
For Aunt Marie he was the second. The first was Joseph,
her beloved brother, wounded in Belgium, transported to
Tours, where he died on May 26, 1916, at the age of
twenty-one.

Once we got that straight, we let her wander in the field
of her archaic memory. Once the principle was established,
there was no need for dialogue. It was strange to hear Rémi
ask her for news of the front and listen to her pessimistic
replies. Sometimes as she looked at him she seemed to be
thinking: the poor boy is out of his mind. She was lost in her
memories. It was hard to follow her because her review of
her past was lacking in continuity. Sometimes when we
thought her preoccupied with the deadly echo of Verdun, it
turned out that she was with us, mourning Father's death.
We would take pleasure in her improvement, glad to have
her sharing our grief, and then there she was again, mourning her own dead: Joseph and Emile, both killed at the front
within a year of each other, and then a sister, Eulalie —

Mathilde was our guide — carried off a year after Emile by the Spanish influenza, not to mention Pierre, the miraculous survivor of 1914, the last brother to be with her, who had died of grief after the death of his wife, Aline. On the subject of Emile, Aunt Marie was the first to speak of Pierre's trip to Commercy, with the imprecation "Buried in secret — like an actor." Here Mathilde was much more discreet and did not seem to understand. She acknowledged the possibility that on this particular point Aunt Marie might be talking nonsense. We, on the other hand, were beginning to take her for a kind of pythoness from whose lips only truths could issue. When it came to reading the past, she was our infallible guide. Still, her answers to our questions came out pell-mell and in the end we were always defeated by the Commercy mystery, as though there were one piece too many in our jigsaw puzzle.

For a time she oscillated between forward and backward, sweeping the century with the beam of her memory. But then she disconnected — a farcical exit embarrassing to those of us who had known her Jansenist constancy. Under the influence of fever, Pascal himself may have made the Périer family laugh with buffooneries that his charitable niece did well to pass over in silence. Nothing would have been remembered but this bit of foolishness, and it would have been used as a means of discrediting the aged infant prodigy with his infinite spaces and eternal silence. And so our aunt's eccentricities made us waver between shock and giggles. Harmless little things like trying for the first time in her life to apply a lipstick from Mathilde's shop, or claiming that Monsieur le curé Bideau was making up to her, or asking for a cigarette and instead of smoking it (which would have been beyond her powers), stowing it behind one ear as a greengrocer does his pencil.

She often asked us to take her back to her mother. With all the diplomacy at our command we tried to explain that her mother might be in no condition to receive her; she refused to listen, and since we hadn't the kindness to escort her, she would go alone. Whereupon she threw on her coat and hat — it was impossible to hold her back — and went wandering about the town, a lost old lady who didn't so much as reply to greetings and fled if anyone spoke to her. Rémi would come out in his car and catch her, and they would drive together in silence, as though looking for an address, two or three times around the square according to the strength of her resistance. Back at the house, Rémi would say they had arrived. She seemed calmed. At other times everything seemed to come back to her; she would say, "Ah yes," and collapse, a crushing reminder that she had not long to live. For a moment her thoughts would stand still, and then her mania would resume control: We must take her back to her mother, we had no idea how terrifying her mother could be if one was late for dinner.

On her last day, Aunt Marie ate her dinner in the company of Rémi and Mathilde, with Pyrrhus at her feet. Meals had taken on the character of a permanent happening, in which Marie, never at a loss, improvised sleight-of-hand tricks with her spoon, put the dog's dish into her plate, repeated for the nth time that her mother wouldn't like it, or rejected a piece of cheese on the ground that it was poisoned. That evening, she grabbed hold of her napkin, plunged it deep into the soup tureen, and spread it out over the television set, which had been turned on. After the moment of stupefaction that always followed her performances, Rémi, who feared a fatal short circuit for his new television set, rushed to the fuse box over the sink and switched off the current. In the darkness we heard the sound of a muffled fall and the barking of the dog. Mathilde groped her way to a candle and lit it. In a flickering chiaroscuro the pale flame disclosed the following fin-de-siècle tableau: Aunt Marie collapsed in her wicker chair, a haggard mater dolorosa, her head covered with a napkin that was irrigating her face and spectacles with strained vegetables that the big tawny spaniel, resting his forepaws on her shoulders, was affectionately lapping up.

Next stop Pont-de-Pitié, the loony bin — as we had called it before this baroque finale.

When things began to look bad for Aunt Marie, Grand-father and Grandmother, fearing one more trial for their daughter (it was less than two months since Father had left us), offered to come and live with us and comfort us in our distress. My mother didn't dare refuse. Loading four enormous suitcases into the 2CV, our grandparents braved the wild ride from Riancé to Random, eighty kilometers of secondary roads through flat, monotonous country with rectangular fields, well-kept hedges, long lines of trees, towns without character, churches without style, houses without pretention, and people without interest. From Riancé to Random the Lower Loire lies hidden in the secret thoughts of its irreproachable wives.

It came as a godsend to see some life, even diminished, getting out of the car. We made haste to help our guests unload their belongings. Zizou removed a bulky suitcase from the backseat and, being neither big enough nor strong enough to carry it, dragged it for six or seven feet: Grand-father was sufficiently vexed to open his mouth and pour cold water on our enthusiasm by telling her to be careful.

At Pont-de-Pitié our Marie had soon sunk into a terminal coma, a long white tunnel that cured her of her last flights of fancy. This was the end, there would be no second miracle. That was why five of us piled into the 2CV to pay her a last visit.

It was late-winter weather, wind and showers, straggling clouds in various shades of gray, and a damp cold that blew through the innumerable cracks in the pathetic vehicle. The four of us had tried in vain to squeeze into the backseat. It's true that Mother didn't take up much room, but in Grandfather's car the arrangement that would have been conceivable in the Citroën DS packed us in like sardines. Grandmother quickly found a solution: she just wouldn't go to Pont-de-Pitié, that was all there was to it; it wasn't as though Marie still had her wits about her. It would be all the same to Marie whether Grandmother came or not. Still, Mother insisted that we children must bestow a last kiss on the aunt who was leaving us. We were getting to be last kiss specialists.

"Kiss your father," she had demanded in the presence of the dressed, cravatted corpse laid out, hands folded, in the middle of the bed, a position symptomatic of the unusual situation, for ordinarily Father slept on the left. The first time there was still a little warmth in him, a certain elasticity in his freshly shaved cheeks. The task was no more difficult than kissing a sleeping baby; you bend down cautiously, you apply a quick kiss, barely time to feel the temperature of the body with the tips of your lips, and there you are, mission accomplished, you go back and huddle around the armchair that Mother has not left. (The second time, just before the body was put into the coffin, when the bowels already had begun to give off a sour smell, we frankly shirked our duty.)

Thus loaded, old Bumpy dragged itself over the wet road. A gust of wind of above-average violence sufficed to halt it in its anemic career. We comforted ourselves with the thought that the wind would be with us on the return trip. But we felt humiliated by those powerful cars (3CV and upward) that passed us as if we were beneath contempt, an excrescence on the shoulder of the road, to be disposed of with a pitying glance or with studied indifference. The most courteous signaled us to move over, and the most charitable jumped up and down in their seats, pretending to be having a hard time passing us. Oh those Good Samaritans of the highway, who splashed us as they sped by, how happy they were to belong to the age of satellites when they passed us prehistoric nomads in our four-wheeled cave.

Squeezed into the backseat, jolted and buffeted, we three would have liked people to think that we had been kid-napped and that the impassive old man at the wheel was not our grandfather. Seated beside him, Mother communed with his silence. She bounced on the bumps like a sad marionette, her face set in a bitter rictus, showing no sign of reproachfulness or irritation but only a grim determination to endure, promising nothing more than to add one second to the last — a prodigious effort beyond which nothing could be asked of her. The bucking of the 2CV detracted somewhat from the dignity of her grief. An abrupt curve obliged her to readjust, without looking, the little black hat pulled low over her forehead, a mere reflex, meaning only that she was still alive. At such moments, however, we sensed that she missed the red DS, which, having become useless for want of a driver, was stored in our garage, awaiting a buyer. The easy suspension that absorbed the bumps, the motor that purred at high speed, the feline acceleration, the 360-degree glass panorama, those com-fortably cushioned seats that relieved the pain in father's back — we hadn't been able to enjoy it for long, barely three months. But in it we were the lords of creation. Pass-ing the 2CV like a roadside flower, Father would have joked about the pathetic vehicle and its occupants, just as when driving through the fog of the Tourmalet Pass he had lightened the atmosphere by remarking on "the white jockey cap" of an intrepid little old man tearing down the blind slope at the wheel of an antique car. Stricken with grief and fallen from our ancient glory, our misery was complete.

The Pont-de-Pitié consists of an old convent and a number of late appendages, built when the convent was transformed into a drying-out center for the drinkers of the region. The main portico with its Roman pediment is wide enough to admit a carriage, but in the courtyard darkened by tall buildings with rain-drenched façades and barred windows, a sense of desolation grips the visitor's throat. The tops of the Lombardy poplars rise above the roofs. The meditative notes of the chapel bell are distorted by the wind. Nuns hurry across the courtyard, slaloming between puddles. When a gust of wind lifts a black skirt, the sister holds it down with both hands, and when the white veil of her wimple flies up and falls back on her eyes, she turns around and for want of hands to remove it, takes a few steps backward into one of the corridors, bordered by wide windows through which falls a mackerel sky. Silicone paint, the smell of incontinent old people which no amount of disinfectant can mask, nauseating kitchen odors (the same eternity-flavored evening soup that is served in school refectories), the busy silhouettes of nuns gliding over the linoleum, patients in pajamas wandering about looking for something — they don't quite know what, and that is what kills them — bewildered glances that betray a thousand torments, a precipitate of distress that no chemistry will ever dissolve, hands clenched, gripping each other like two links in a broken chain, hesitant, frightened gait, frenzied words, abrupt, demented movements, and in the cloister the hard-core loonies, the clones of Napoleon and Louis XIV, the Anastasias and apocryphal princesses out of an imaginary Almanach de Gotha, fabulous dynasties of the kingdom of fools. A race of imposters that our sovereign Virgin Marie did not have to put up with for long.

We felt cramped in the tiny room with its white walls and furniture, but stayed as far as possible from the bed placed facing the window, through which we could see the wind torturing the poplars. We dared go no closer for fear of colliding with the drip-feed bottles or getting tangled up in the tubes if we bent over the tiny, deathly pale body with the frail, diaphanous arms, so frail, so transparent as they lay on the sheet that we understood our aunt had chosen to slip gently away rather than die. Without her glasses, her face blended with the pallor of the pillowcase; what was left of her body made a minimal depression in the sheets, the barest wrinkle of life connected with the world by transparent tubes, soon to be smoothed out by a breath from another world.

Mother seemed out of place in her mourning. We were standing at the edge of a hole in the universe into which the world of appearances was slowly emptying. We almost stopped breathing, diluted ourselves in this vanishing spring. The nuns, ordinarily so brusque with their charges, entered on tiptoe for fear of disturbing the sleep of the blessed one. Mother, who had been showing signs of impatience, took advantage of a moment when one of the sisters was busying herself with the patient, to give the signal for departure. We left the dying wraith without a farewell kiss.

Back at the house, Grandfather took refuge in the attic. Since moving in with us for humanitarian reasons, he had assigned himself two functions, beyond which nothing more could be asked of him: shopping ("Monsieur Burgaud" was soon well known to the shopkeepers, who complimented him on his devotion) and reorganizing the attic, his own idea, which occupied his afternoons. To put it bluntly, the shopping to get out of the house, the attic to be unmolested. He also took on another duty, which spoiled his visit and hastened its end: to supply the authority of the parent we had lost and to further the education of Zizou, who soon became his "whipping boy." She should not: put her elbows on the table, chew with her mouth open, bang on her plate with her spoon, or interrupt; she should: wait to be spoken to, etc. Immured in her grief, Mother noticed nothing. It was Nina who, perceiving her little sister's plight from the lofty vantage point of her fourteen years, summoned Grandfather and Grandmother to her presence on the day of Aunt Marie's death and notified them that they were expected to leave immediately after the funeral. If Mother was ever aware of her elderly parents' presence in the house, she must still be wondering what made them leave.

For Grandfather shopping was a way of stocking up secretly on the sweets that had been forbidden him ever since his blood had been found to contain an excess of glucose, not enough to necessitate a daily injection of insulin — a circumstance that made us suspicious of his supposed diabetes — but enough to make him resign him-

self, with Grandmother's help, to replacing the usual eight
lumps of sugar in his coffee with saccharine tablets, which
were far from giving him the same pleasure. All his life he
had consoled himself in this way, as unhappy people often
do. Formerly he had bought his sweets loose by the quarter
pound, and he would never have let anyone choose them
for him. He went to Nantes now and then to buy cloth, and
he had an address there, on the rue de Verdun near the
cathedral, of an old-fashioned grocery shop, dark, a sort of
colonial anomaly, dating from the days of the city's murky
splendor, smelling predominantly of coffee beans, tea, and
spices and as chockful of exotic merchandise as a South Sea
Islands trading post. Glass jars were lined up on three
shelves in the entrance. It was hard to choose amid the
extraordinary variety of humbugs, caramels, honey and
menthol lozenges, green cough drops, chocolate nuggets,
pistachio, violet, or marshmallow pastilles, licorice sticks,
and so on. Grandfather's dream was to help himself, to
plunge the little triangular copper scoop into the middle of
these marvels, but the pasty-faced owners, smug in their
gray smocks, never allowed him to. It was their trade and
indeed they had an eye for it. By sheer guesswork they came
within a few grams of the correct weight; they had only to
add one or two pieces to balance their gigantic Roberval
scale. This precision was the glory of their métier. It would
have been unjust to prevent them from exercising a talent
they had paid for with a hundred years in the grocery trade.

Grandfather came out with his little white bags carefully
sealed with Scotch tape. On arriving at Riancé he emptied
them into a cylindrical jar, decorated with rococo designs,
tucked away at the top of the sideboard beyond the reach of
the grandchildren. His hiding place was a secret to no one,
but was part of a ritual. After waiting for us to leave the

kitchen, he would reach in and take a good handful for the day, which made his pockets sticky and threw Grandmother into a rage. We would hear the sound of a chair being dragged over the tile floor. Rather than change his hiding place, he preferred this bit of childish-geriatric gymnastics, as good a way as any of making time stand still.

Since he could not smoke in his tailor's shop with its bolts of material, since his hands were busy with his work and he kept a row of pins between his lips during fitting sessions, he compensated by sucking sweets. While his worn face concentrated on his needle, we could hear the soft flow of saliva and the contractions of his throat. At such times, the slightly arrogant expression he had with his cigarette between his lips disappeared and his little slit eyes took on a look of what might have been taken for resignation.

But here in our house he repaired to the attic after his siesta. From time to time we interpreted a sound as a piece of furniture being dragged, another as a mini landslide, and still another as a breaking of glass, and we worried. But most of the time we listened in vain — he seemed to have fallen asleep. Grandmother couldn't conceal her anxiety: what could he be doing up there? Could he have found another Ile du Levant in our junk pile? We were dying to go up and see, but for us the attic was off-limits. Not expressly. Nothing had actually been said, but you just didn't disturb Grandfather in his domain. His silence, his way of looking at you without seeing you out of eyes half closed behind the smoke of his cigarette, created a forbidden zone around him that none of us dared cross without his consent. He would come down an hour before dinner with cobwebs in his hair and dust on his jacket, brush his clothes carefully, rectify the crease in his trousers by passing it between his two fingers (Grandmother had vainly suggested a more appropriate costume), and insist on our washing our hands at the same time as he did.

One evening Grandmother ventured to ask him a few questions about his activities up there. He did not answer directly but asked Mother if she knew what had happened in Commercy. Mother looked up, surprised that anyone should be addressing a living corpse. Grandfather did not insist. But one Sunday he sounded out Mathilde over the hedge between the two gardens. She waved her hand as though to wipe away something she wanted to hear no more about.

Thereupon Aunt Marie died. We noted that it was March 19, Saint Joseph's Day, as though she had studied the calendar every day of her unconscious travels and arranged to disembark on the one day that to her mind united her recently deceased nephew and the distant memory of her brother.

A wild wind was blowing on the day of the funeral. It lifted surplices as well as women's skirts. Several altar boys clutched the staff of the tall black and silver banner, which, buffeted by the wind, twisted, furled, swelled, and tried to take flight. At the head of the procession the Cross bearer charged into the tempest, leveling his bronze crucifix like a halberd. The curé Bideau, unable to keep his stole over his shoulder, tied it around his neck like a scarf, its gold embroidery glittering as it floated behind him. The wind turned the pages of his missal faster than he could read them. For fear of tearing the fine Bible paper, he shut the book and improvised his prayers. The hymns he struck up at the top of his voice were swallowed by the gale and were on their way to Paris before the choir had time to join in. The altar boy responsible for the holy water had already spilled half of the precious liquid on his cassock. When it came time for the asperges, we shared what was left, the aspergillum being dipped purely pro forma. The howling of the wind drowned out the footfalls of the procession; we advanced with our heads down, fighting for each breath, trusting the marcher ahead of us to lead in the right direction, our main concern being to avoid flying away. Grandmother and Mother had removed their veils; Grandfather held his hat firmly in one hand; others were running after berets or scarves. Drawn by Monsieur Biloche's horse, the hearse pitched and rolled, its black draperies flapping like a flock of crows. On the long curve leading to the cemetery it almost capsized (this was its last voyage; from then on an ambulance transported the dead). The younger Biloche judged that we could go no farther without endangering the security of the deceased. He chose three strong men in the cortege. Together, they took hold of the coffin, pulled it out from under its canopy, and after exchanging a glance hoisted it vigorously onto their shoulders with an ease that startled them. Their starting heave was too powerful for the featherweight they were carrying, and the coffin came close to leaping into the air like a volunteer being tossed on a blanket at the firemen's carnival. Thus it was on the shoulders of men, wedged firmly against their cheeks, rolling perhaps in a receptacle too big for her that our Virgin Marie crossed the threshold of her last resting place, like a queen, her soul blushing that such handsome men should hallow her timid womanhood by carrying it on their shoulders.

On our return from the cemetery, Grandfather went up to the attic for the last time, just long enough to pick up a shoe box that he brought down and handed to Mother with a few words of explanation. Mother listened wearily and, not knowing where to put the box, left it on a corner of the writing desk, where it soon disappeared under a pile of papers. The old people loaded their suitcases into the 2CV — quick kisses good-bye on the sidewalk outside the shop (Grandfather's prickly mustache, Grandmother's softer one), a display of emotion not quite concealing feelings of good riddance on both sides and a general sense of fiasco. The car had scarcely vanished around the bend when we rushed upstairs to inspect the new order in the attic.

The place was hardly recognizable. On the supposition that order is only a subjective variation on disorder, it can be said that the attic as rearranged by Grandfather was the same as before, but that for our chaos he had substituted another, the only difference being that the new one was unfamiliar. On the shelves where in the course of time precious waste products of civilization had accumulated, constituting a stratigraphic record of successive generations and their elementary concept of survival, Grandfather, by modifying the spectrum of this accumulation, had scrambled time and shuffled the cards of our family Pincevent. In this new dispensation all our benchmarks had vanished. With the same elements he had composed a different picture, a different history. Now we would have to get used to this redistribution of memory, to the little blue ceramic man in the canary's cage, to the string of black beads around the neck of the one-armed teddy bear, who would have got his arm back again if Father had mastered the skills of a seamstress, to the bronze candlesticks supporting a pile of seventy-eights (including some of a certain Bach's comic barrack-room stories), to a disorderly pile of magazines in the wicker cradle, all carrying the same undying recipe for *blanquette de veau,* to the broken mirror on the dust-gray floor with its fragmentary reflections of rafters, to the orphaned shoe resting on a carefully tied-up packet of bills, attesting for a thousand years that they have actually been paid, not to mention countless other objects that had reappeared from nowhere, such as that tin pipette, that conical brass projectile, that Chinese hat with little holes in it like a colander, that snake-shaped implement, this judiciously compartmented wooden chest. For the upheaval had brought to light not only objects that had been hidden away and forgotten, but also, apparently, some that no one had ever seen before.

Among other things, Grandfather had disinterred a series of photographic portraits that he had lined up facing the Voltaire armchair in which he must have sat (witness the ashtray full of cigarette butts next to a chair leg). He had not classified them according to any genealogical principle but had grouped them on the basis of resemblances, morphological affinities as it were, as though trying with the help of a theory of reincarnation to trace the passage of life from generation to generation and, guided by this red thread of similarities, to devise a recipe for immortality. Confronted by these fragments of ourselves dispersed among long-past and largely unknown faces, we could not deny that we were an enduring part of them. In the eyes of one remote ancestress (in a quasi-daguerreotype) we recognized, intact, the eyes of Zizou. That gaze transmitted across death was upsetting.

There was still the shoe box. That solemn transfer, those few words murmured in secret. It was evident that Grandfather had confided his most essential finds to the shoe box. We shook it. It didn't clink. Even if there was no gold in it, at least it would bring us proof of some glorious ancestry.

In it were some photographs, postcards, and letters, a brooch, a medallion, and two notebooks. The writing in the more battered of the two got worse as one turned the pages.

Toward the end it became almost illegible, a few scrawled notes gradually merging with the whiteness of the last blank pages. In the photos we recognized Father's parents: Pierre in his car or in uniform, Aline massive in an armchair, with a little black-and-white dog on her lap, or as a smiling young girl. All the documents related to those two, with the exception of a religious picture such as we might have expected to find in Aunt Marie's missal. But on closer scrutiny, the prayer on the back had a pronounced patriotic accent. It had to do with the Great War, in which God had unmistakably sided with the eldest daughter of the Church. With such backing the outcome could not be in doubt. Joseph, Marie's eldest brother, would unquestionably have rejoiced, but a handwritten note confirmed that he had died of his wounds at Tours, on May 26, 1916. We put the picture on the sideboard and at Nina's suggestion replaced it in the shoe box with the gold denture and the two wedding rings.

What is there inside a nut? The imagination runs wild: Ali Baba's cave? The wood of the True Cross? Rudolph Valentino's voice? You crack it and eat it. You learn that it contains trace elements and vitamins, glucides and lipids, but that Ali Baba's cave is in the head of Scheherazade, the wood of the True Cross in the Tree of Knowledge, and Rudolph Valentino's voice in the deaf man's glance.

III

OUR AUNT MARIE MIGHT almost have regarded the Byzantine divines who argued about the sex of the angels as pornographers. Even Father felt uncomfortable when we asked him (we were waiting in the car outside the maternity hospital while Mother paid a visit from which children were excluded) how among those little lumps of pink flesh the boys could be distinguished from the girls. He hesitated a moment, tapping the steering wheel with his fingers, in him a sign of irritation. Phallus, penis? Too scientific. Member? Dull. Pecker? Childish (a child is no longer a child). Then came sudden illumination. Turning to us with a mischievous, embarrassed smile: "Watering can." What a wonderful, modest father.

Further information on the subject was not forthcoming, and we had no end of trouble later on when we discovered the dual function of the watering can. Still, it did the job. The arrow trembled for a moment but nevertheless penetrated the bull's eye. The aura of silence surrounding the swollen belly of expectant mothers is a way of emphasizing the absurdity of the nebula that makes us take so cautious, almost detached an attitude toward it — as though life had little to do with us or we with life.

Yet innuendos come to light now and then. Witness, in the shoe box, the "book of songs" kept by Aline as a young girl ("this notebook belongs to . . . ," signed by her), in which, along with "La Paimpolaise" by the Breton bard Théodore Botrel, "I have two big oxen in my barn," "You're much too little, sonny" ("sixteen years old and no bigger than . . ."), we suddenly come across "an object of desire which stretches and grows longer and which, you've guessed it, ladies, is nothing other than a garter." This misapprehension, sustained up to the last line, may have coaxed from the luncheon guests something resembling a sigh of relief, soon drowned out by "I know of a church not far from here, You'll see the steeple reflected in the mere."

Somehow, perhaps in connection with Nina's first period (for it was Nina who told us about it), our old Aunt Marie managed to confide that her menstrual history represented a parenthesis of eight years in her life — from her eighteenth (hardly a mark of precocity) to her twenty-sixth year — an aberration of nature in that frail body, as though to leave less room for erotic stirrings in one whose energies would henceforth be devoted to the imitation of the saints and the education of children: two thousand little girls over fifty years, three generations, as many republics, and two world wars, and she was still praying with her pupils for peace in Algeria.

She took her pedagogical talent as a debt to the Lord, an apostolate, a responsibility: no fig tree must remain without fruit. Thus she succeeded in teaching a dejected, virtually autistic woman of forty to read, write, and count. This woman rather frightened us when we were sent to order "a chicken for five" from her farmer parents. Sitting between wall and sideboard, in a dark corner of the kitchen, the red cardigan over her emaciated shoulders seeming to consume her like a flaming tunic, she sways her head gently back and forth to the rhythm of her monotone thoughts and the creaking of the wicker. Her whole body appears to be like a clock; as though her sole purpose in living were to measure the term of her life. Sometimes she tightens the collar of her cardigan around her neck and shivers as though struck by a wave of cold from within. Her face, always inclined, is hidden under a mass of hair that accompanies her perpetual motion. Her felt slippers are too big for her, her stockings are bunched up, and one of her feet is always on top of the other. She never looks us in the eye, and when we greet her she answers with a grunt. If our visit does not necessitate her mother's presence, she takes a notebook out of a drawer in the sideboard and writes down our order in a hesitant, laborious hand that has something miraculous about it, recalling the disjointed walk of a "cured" paraplegic, whose every step is a victory over impending disaster. If she doesn't happen to be sticking her tongue out, this is how you must see her: bent over her page of writing, almost lying on her left arm, which along with her hair cuts off our view of her face, a permanent apprentice delivering words like pain-ridden babies buried in the thickness of the paper. Then, her task accomplished, her features showing no sign of distress or triumph but only of absence; she shuts the notebook, returns notebook and pencil to the drawer, and still with lowered head goes back to her chair, a signal for us to leave, to abandon her to her chasms, a gloomy descent that makes the cedar-lined lane leading to the highway seem like an avenue of celestial light. It is true that she learned to give us the right change. Her parents were so proud, so grateful to Aunt Marie, that they never failed to slip a few eggs from their farm into our basket.

Marie's success may have gone to her head, or perhaps it was because of her certainty that God was on her side that she tried her talents on little Annie. But there she had to give up. Ageless, with a big smiling face and the slit eyes of her mental Mongolia, little Annie roamed the streets in a schoolgirl's smock, her white socks pulled up to her knees, her neatly combed hair held in place by a barrette. Proud of her pretty ribbons, she saw herself as a beauty queen and, when anyone asked how she was getting along, invariably replied, like a Jew exiled far from Jerusalem, "Little Annie in Paris tomorrow." Her wish in the end was granted: Reuniting the diaspora of her chromosomes, she was to die in Paris above her elder sister's pastry shop in Passy. Did she, like the newcomer who looks for Rome in Rome and in Rome fails to see Rome, inform the inhabitants of the capital's better neighborhoods, who may be less indulgent than we in the provinces, that she would be going to Paris tomorrow? Paris was the one word that she identified, thanks to a trick of Aunt Marie, who in place of the letter A drew an Eiffel Tower, so that little Annie, when confronted with the life-size monument, was no doubt the only one among millions of visitors to read the name of the promised city in the network of girders.

Poor aunt, one can imagine the childlike tone of forced playfulness she must have put on when joining in the conversation without being invited. Actually, she was vexed that no one paid any attention to her, when she had something to say on every subject. (This exasperated Father; it was beyond him how she could form an opinion of such and such a soccer player. Even when snubbed she would make us repeat the name in preparation for a future discussion, in the course of which she would refer to him as if he were an old friend.) But that day the topic was not right for her. Actually, she dreaded it like the plague — all this joining of bodies and conception of babies, a subject which, thanks to the judicious primness of the day, she was never obliged to teach. Nevertheless, rather than stay on her island all by herself, she plunged bravely into the water, contributing what she knew of the question, her modest experience, that humble stone in the edifice of knowledge.

If it hadn't been for Nina, no one would have paid attention to her. And so, nettled by our lack of interest in her remarks, our old aunt informed us once again, as though adding an important document to a sensitive file, that as far as she was concerned the problem of sex had been solved for good at the age of twenty-six and that far from grieving her, her amenorrhea was the best thing that could have happened to her — a good riddance to that bothersome monthly reminder of her womanhood, a kind of divine grace enabling her, purified in body and soul, to build on the ruins of her life as a woman the limpid destiny of a saintly teacher for the glory of God on high.

Of course we teased her a little, expressing surprise that she had never married. She claimed that the choice had rested entirely with her, there had been plenty of suitors, about whom, despite our insistence, she would tell us absolutely nothing. But in view of her arid grayness, we felt sure they must have been dismal enough to justify her choice to remain an immaculate unmarried mother of forty children a year.

Just once she is caught in an act of coquetry, at the wedding of our father and mother. A picture of the procession shows her on Grandfather's arm, as smart as can be in a long black sheath, a broad-brimmed hat tilted over one ear, black gloves, and black handbag, her chin thrust out proudly from her worn little face, but her hair already white. This sublime swan song in honor of her nephew could not efface thirty years of renunciation, of self-abnegation. Already she has that look of a little old woman that she must have adopted at twenty-six. How is one to imagine her running from shop to shop, choosing a dress, looking at her black-sheathed self in the mirror, running her hands over her pathetic figure? More likely, she owed

her outfit to Grandfather, who indeed dressed a good part
of the wedding. But, apparently in seventh heaven, she does
not try to hide from the photographer. She carries her head
tilted to one side in the posture we have always known and
that we made fun of in a friendly kind of way. That was her
true self, her mark, and years later, when we saw Mo-
digliani's women, we were rather disappointed that from
this same tilt other women should derive a glory that was
hers by right. Surely there can be no harm in a little flurry of
elegance, a little spurt of audacity once in a lifetime. Especially since she can't help suspecting that the flattering
looks, the marks of interest, are addressed not to her but to
the head of the procession. She knows that she lacks the
Parisian distinction of Grandfather, who wears his morning
coat with an aristocratic flair acquired through close contact with the masters. One senses that she is prepared at the
first contretemps to go back to her shapeless skirts, her
battered black shopping bag, and her little house in our
garden, and once the parenthesis of this glorious day is
closed, to resume the countdown of her last menstruation
at the age of twenty-six. If for once we count with her
instead of affecting to be bored with her stories, our count-
ing, since she was born in 1890, will to our surprise bring us
to the year 1916 and, with a little more precision, to the
month of May, when her brother Joseph breathed his last.

So this was what she was telling us when disclosing her
cabalistic calculations to no one in particular. That long,
secret repression of grief, that blood checked as one checks
tears, and through this death her life forever thrown off
course.

The first use of poison gas in warfare had occurred the year before. It happened to the north of Ypres in Belgium, and for that reason the gas was named yperite. It did not make its inventor proud enough to want his name attached to it, as Pasteur's is to pasteurization or Lecoq's to gallium (from *gallus*, "cock"); thus there is nothing Gallic about the appellation at which German chemists took such umbrage that fifty years later, in reprisal, they gave the name "germanium" to a new metallic element. This propensity for annexing place names, this *über alles*, should have aroused our suspicions. In the secrecy of the laboratory, testing his chlorine cocktails on defenseless animals, the heartless gas man — in whose research the future death camps were implicit — was not unaware that he was contravening The Hague conventions whereby countries in the habit of fighting one another had agreed, with a view to keeping the costs down, to wage the next war correctly, in accordance with the mystique of chivalry and the principle of the duel, a planetary version of the Battle of the Thirty, where the foes would slay one another on a battlefield covering three departments, never overstepping the sidelines of the lists nor injuring the multitude of villains, whom such princely jousts have never concerned. But that was in peacetime when healthy people think of themselves as reasonable patients. Try asking Joseph, with his scorched lungs, not to howl with pain. For months now the thirty have been millions, decimated, exhausted, a colony of the living dead dug into the mud of the Somme and Marne regions, flung groggy with sleep into murderous counterattacks to capture a hill that will be lost tomorrow. Entire divisions are being massacred, pawns moved about on general-staff maps by lunatic Nivelles, Schlieffen Plan versus Plan XVII, a tête-à-tête between stags immobilized by each other's antlers. In the present quarrel of surveyors, rules of warfare, so precious at Fontenoy under the last of the condottieri, led to astronomical death tolls and total bestiality. The expense was staggering. The little chemist's suggestion looked like good business: a kilogram of explosive cost two marks forty, whereas a kilogram of chlorine cost eighteen pfennigs and caused greater ravages. In view of the billions being made by the steel barons, it was simple if you shut your eyes to the side effects; victory on the cheap.

Thus it came about that Joseph saw a greenish dawn rising over the Ypres plain. God, that morning, was with the enemy. The complicit wind pushed the green mist toward the French lines. It clung to the ground, hugging every rise and fall in the terrain, plunging into hollows, swallowing hillocks and barbed-wire entanglements, an engulfing tide, comparable to the waters of the Red Sea that swallowed up the chariots of Pharaoh's army.

The officer gave orders to open fire. This must be a smokescreen, he thought, dissimulating a large-scale attack. It is doubtful whether men had ever before fired at the wind. The shooting relieved the tension but failed to impede the inexorable advance of the seething, bubbling flow. Now it was almost close enough to touch, men looked up with eyes of amazement, and raised futile arms to ward it off, wondering what new monstrosity had been invented to torment them with. The first wisps of gas penetrated the trench.

That was that. Earth ceased to be the magnificent blue ball that can be wondered at from outer space. Above Ypres a horrible greenish spot spread. Oh, admittedly the methane dawn of the world's first days was not exactly hospitable, the blue for which we are envied, the diffracted sunlight as we see it, is no more eternal than our lives. According to nature's seasons and man's inclemency, it will veer to purple or saffron, but this pistachio tinge along the Yser betokened an evil intention. Now the chlorinated fog infiltrates the network of communications trenches, seeps into dugouts (mere sections of trench covered with planks), nestles in potholes, creeps through the rudimentary partitions of casemates, plunges into underground chambers hitherto preserved from shells, pollutes food and water supplies, occupies space so methodically that frantic pain-racked men search vainly for a breath of air. The first reflex was to bury your head in your jacket, but the bit of oxygen that gives you is exhausted in three breaths. Out comes your head, you hold your breath as long as you can, before inhaling the horrible mixture. We have never really listened to those elderly twenty-year-olds, whose testimony would help us to retrace the paths of horror: the intolerable burning in the eyes, nose, and throat, the suffocating pain in the chest, the violent cough that tears the lungs and the pleura and brings bloody froth to the lips, the acrid vomiting that doubles up the body, the fallen whom death will soon garner, trampled by their stronger comrades trying with their hands on the edge of the trench to hoist themselves out of it, to escape from this swarm of human worms, but their feet get tangled up in the telephone wires stapled to the parapet, and the resulting landslide uncovers tatters of last autumn's summarily buried bodies. Once above ground, men struggle desperately through the green mist and the fetid mud. Suddenly a leg is sucked into a hole in the soft

clay, the effort of pulling it out racks the lungs. Men fall
into putrid puddles, their hands and feet coated with freez-
ing mud, their bodies shaken by burning rales. And then,
once out of the caustic green mist — O fresh transparent
air — the time-honored methods of warfare take over,
and the survivors are raked by an intense bombardment.
Only the luckiest reach the second line. Joseph is one of
these — or else he is picked up not too far forward to be
saved by a greathearted buddy. But his condition is
alarming — deep lesions, and one lung probably will have
to be removed. He is put down for transfer to Tours, which
is not a good sign. He sees himself headed for home; for him
the war is over. He even finds the strength to acquiesce
when others envy his condition. Those of sound body and
no knowledge would gladly give a lung at the thought of the
women who will be coddling him.

For the present a regiment of Moroccans is sent to reoc-
cupy the lost positions. The gas has not cleared away, but
desert people are used to sandstorms, which also sting the
eyes and lungs.

The trip to Touraine is long. To keep the jolting to a
minimum, the convoy moves slowly. Improvised ambu-
lances, rudimentary springs, rough roads, potholes — the
groans of the wounded. Joseph is impatient. Now that we
know how it's going to end for him, it would be better to
pile up the miles indefinitely to delay his arrival as long as
possible. But his pain is unbearable. Chartres, Châteaudun,
Vendôme. We'll be there soon.

Feverish, disjointed words, faces convulsed with terror
betray the hallucinated memory of such visions of hell;
half-buried corpses, torn, dismembered bodies on barbed
wire, blue starlings caught in a net and apparently denied
the ultimate comfort of lying down, of waiting with their

cheeks to the damp ground for death to deliver them, shaken with grotesque spasms when hit by stray bullets, lifted like straw dolls by the blast of an explosion, flying as in Icarus's disjointed dream through a sky traversed by lightning bolts before embracing the fertile muck for the last time; mouths locked open by terror, eyes wide with amazement that so much trouble is being taken. Meanwhile, the overturned helmet fills with clear water saved from the mire, delicate birdbath for the day of peace. But the birds have deserted the thundering sky rent with flaming parabolas — except, now and then, for the poor pigeons, released into the tempest with secret messages on which soldiers concentrate their fire, relieved to be shooting pigeons (though of a different species) as they might be doing at home. From the opposite trenches a cry of childish joy is heard when a messenger cut off in its flight falls heavily, and then we curse them as never before, because suddenly it occurs to us that the fallen bird was carrying the solution to all our misery.

Landscape of lamentation, bare ground sown and enriched by these plowman's bodies, bristling black stumps commemorating a shady grove, nation of mud, shapeless clay of a human creation given back to matter with its vanities, putrid muck mingled with the acrid smell of burned powder and slaughtered flesh that makes one's own stench (weeks without undressing) almost bearable. With the wind that, when the din dies down, transmits the groans of the dying in silence, engraves them like prophetic messages in the flesh of the mute, prostrate survivors listening to those amputated lives. With the night, which is not a pause of the heart, not that ineffably sensuous peace, but a place of expectancy, of suspended death and blackened faces, of sentries found at dawn with their throats cut, of guilty sleep. With day, announced by artillery fire, prelude to an offensive, and, there is reason to fear, destined to end before its time. With interminable rain that washes the original taint again and again, transforms the earth into a swamp, floods shell holes, drowning the heavily encumbered soldiers, the rain that streams through the trenches, flattens sandbag bulwarks, infiltrates collars and shoes, weighs down uniforms, liquefies bones, penetrates to the center of the earth, as though the world were reduced to a sponge, an infernal swamp for souls in pain. And finally the rain on the convoy, gently tapping on the roof of the ambulance, suddenly grown soothing, almost friendly, transformed by headlight beams into thousands of fireflies, beads of moonlight that bounce rhythmically on the road, traverse dark cities, and, approaching Tours at daybreak, glide into the riverbed at the foot of the royal flower gardens of old France.

Joseph will not die. His sister Marie has taken the trip from Random to Tours with a supply of pious medals. No sooner does she arrive than she slips them under the pillows of her brother and his companions in misery, taking advantage of moments when the white-aproned nurses, who move from bed to bed with the grace of Russian ballerinas, have their backs turned. Some of the nurses, who believe only in science and its Cartesian virtues, are infuriated by these grigris — a shipment of morphine would do more good. For morphine, that kindly substance, is in short supply. Subjected to pleas from all sides, they dose it carefully, distributing it according to empirical criteria: intensity of pain, proximity of death. When none is available, they want to stop their ears and scream louder than all this accumulated pain. This war is going too far. All agree that it will be the last. For Joseph and millions of others, it certainly will.

At her brother's bedside Marie sets to work without delay. She takes out her rosary, searches her heaven, and chooses the head of the pain department — it is Christ himself, though the martyred, dismembered, stoned, and scalded saints are not undeserving — and with rosary after rosary implores him to take on his sturdy carpenter's shoulders the additional burden of her brother's heaving, whistling chest. In exchange — she wonders what she might give him, for she has nothing to give but herself — very well, she will give him the desire that invades her entrails at night, she will give him her woman's blood. Blood for blood, it's an honest bargain. And true enough, Joseph's cheeks take on color, he sits up in bed and asks for food. It is spring in

Touraine, the Loire is swollen with melted snow, the last sprigs of lily of the valley are there in a glass. He speaks of going home soon, makes a show of high spirits, teases one of the nurses, promises to marry her when he gets well. She laughs (it's at least her twentieth proposal), Marie reacts with a tightlipped smile. Then he feels tired again, coughs a little, wants to rest. He stretches out with his arms at his sides, shuts his eyes. After his short remission, the rales, the fever, the visions of horror resume. At nightfall he is deathly pale. Now the doctor offers no hope. The young fiancée passes at regular intervals in the half-light and quietly, so as not to disturb those who are sleeping, puts a fresh compress on his forehead and pulls the sheets up over his chest. When a violent coughing fit makes him sit up, she takes him in her arms like a child and inserts a spoonful of cough syrup between his lips. At dawn the immense ward is flooded with light, the splashing of the river is heard through the silence. There is a frightening fixity in his eyes. Marie, the first visitor to arrive, is aghast. It's not yet the end, they tell her, but she must be prepared. His eyes are softer when death comes in the middle of the afternoon.

Joseph's death is a matter of public record — his name appears on a pious, patriotic picture on sale for five centimes (proceeds to charity) at the Commercy (subprefecture of the Meuse department, specialty: madeleines) presbytery, framed in a narrow black border, the very epitome of sorrow, bearing the title of a heroic novel, "Fields of Glory," and a subtitle for a pulp edition: "Where the blood of France flowed in rivers from 1914 to 1916." (The battle is still in progress. A booklet dealing with everything that happened here is announced for after the war.) A large black cross with the monogram of Christ in its center is surrounded by the names of the tragic battlefields: Artois,

Serbia, Dardanelles, Marne, Meuse, Lorraine, Alsace, Argonne, Yser, a crown of horror listing, on a screen of olive branches, the subgroup of martyred towns assessed according to magnitude of slaughter, so that Vimy is written as large as Lens, Dixmude as large as Ostende, Les Eparges as Nancy. "May this picture remind us all of the gratitude we owe to God for the prodigious battle of the Marne and for the solidity of our front since then." And if, as written, the battle was that prodigious, in a class with the cross of Clovis in the sky at Tolbiac, with Saint Geneviève delivering Paris, with Joan of Arc delivering Orléans, and Leo I persuading the Vandal Genseric to spare the lives of the inhabitants of Rome, God may also have been with us — a Father heartbroken that His sons should make such use of their freedom, yet preserving the same sorrowful love for each and every one.

"In pious memory of the heroes, in particular of . . ." — fill in the name — a rivulet flowing into the great red river, the *cloaca maxima,* the menstrual she-wolf. This is done in her impeccable hand by his sister Marie, then a young schoolteacher, who has lost two brothers in this segment of history (the official variety, which for once coincides with our own neglected chronicle) and adds in the margin, since there is room only for the name, which has to be short (it is a form for commoners, the rank and file, who figure at length on the war memorials sculptured in the style of the Deposition from the Cross, thus burdening the lists of the fallen with the full weight of a certain republican concept of salvation): "Age 21, wounded in Belgium died in Tours, May 26, 1916." And this brief commentary saves Joseph from the long amnesiac night.

Between these two limits, on this dotted line, Aunt Marie, in time-diluted violet ink, sets down the mystery to be elucidated concerning a life that has ended. Age twenty-one. We know, since she taught us as much, that La Pérouse commanded a frigate at the age of fourteen, so that seven years later he undoubtedly had the memories of an old sea dog. Joseph, on the other hand, who left his native village to die, saw only a devastated landscape and, on his travels, only the sordid anonymity of cattle cars and an ambulance tarpaulin above his damaged eyes. Joseph, who may never have known pleasure with a woman, Joseph catapulted into a human hell. Joseph, too young for this major act, "Joseph," as she wrote, "died May 26, 1916."

A year later it was Emile's turn. That difference of one year would separate the two brothers on the war memorial's interminable list: Joseph in the 1916, Emile in the 1917 column. Thus exiled from each other, a curious visitor, struck by their homonymy, might have mistaken them for mere cousins — whereas their two names in the same column would have united them in death, giving rise to a vision of two brothers fallen side by side, swept away by the same explosion, forever twinned by memory. Marie shared her grief over this second death, for which she had only her tears to give, with Mathilde, Emile's young widow and the mother of little Rémi, whom his father discovered during a short leave granted him for the birth. Entering the room in uniform at nightfall, he tiptoes over to the cradle and bends down cautiously, for fear of disturbing the little sleeping creature with the turmoil of the war. Suddenly Emile is struck dumb with joy by those tiny fists clenched over pleasant dreams, the fine-spun hair, the delicately hemmed line of the closed eyes, the transparent network of the veins, the indescribable freshness of the child's breath on his bruised hand. Lifting the muslin netting, Mathilde presents her creation to her great man. For that is how she sees him in his bedraggled uniform, which smells of sweat, dust, and the misery of war. In his hardened features, the unfamiliar creases around his mouth and on his forehead, she reads the harshness of his life out there and his unflagging inner courage. To him, whose whole existence is one of privation, she doesn't dare speak of her privations here at home, of the rough man's jobs she has to do, the decisions she has to take

alone, of her fatigue, of this last joyless Christmas without
him, of the little crèche which, in spite of everything, she set
up on the chest of drawers, with its wrapping paper that
was supposed to look like a mountain and transformed that
little corner of Palestine into a Paleolithic cave. She feels full
of gratitude and compassion. Resting her hand on the back
of his neck, she tells him how cruelly she has missed their
tenderness, while he, raising his head from the cradle, feels
the soft perfume of this powdered woman going to his
head. She has waited so long she cannot be sure that this is
the man for whom she has been yearning desperately.
Looking at him now as he stands beside her, she wonders if
she didn't overestimate his size when, hugging herself in a
sham embrace, she tried, for the sweater she was knitting,
to conjure up her husband's torso, with this resting place
for her head, this specially designed hollow in his shoulder,
which she now tries to find with her forehead. Meanwhile,
he is pulling out her hairpins one by one with the skill of a
hunter of lice, putting them down on the bedside table,
where she will be able to find them when dressing in the
morning, after he has handed her the baby, who has
woken up crying. Set down on his mother, he starts sucking avidly, milky tears flowing from his mouth. Once the
child is sated, his father lifts him up at arm's length in the
pale light of day, at the risk of a white flood that will soil
the blue uniform laid out on the chair. But Emile doesn't
let that worry him. He feels miraculously invulnerable for
the battles to come, as sure as an Indian ghost dancer of
passing through the gunfire, fortified by the memory of
this victorious child born on December 2, the anniversary
of the battle of Austerlitz and of Napoleon's Coronation,
a sign of nobody knew exactly what, but which Rémi
never failed to mention on his birthday, sprinkling himself

meanwhile with a little Imperial Mist. Thus the last kiss Emile gave his son before returning to the front to die became confused with the Fontainebleau farewells in a room papered with heraldic bees.

Emile wasn't present at his funeral. For years Mathilde mourned beside an empty grave. Her husband was definitely dead, his body had been identified, but at the end the fighting was so fierce that the truce necessary for the stretcher bearers to do their job was no longer respected. Every major offensive was preceded by an artillery bombardment that was likely to last for as much as eight days, during which enough explosives to wipe an entire country off the map would descend on the area to be softened up. The poor soldiers, burrowed deep in the ground, deafened by the din, unable to stretch out an arm to grab a water bottle, went hungry for days before the arrival of a field kitchen (those unarmed heroes who precariously hauled enormous cauldrons and sacks full of bread through the communications trenches), sleeping watchfully in a hole in the ground, certain that the whole world to the very end would consist of nothing but this concentrated horror. Little by little, abandoned corpses sank into the clay, slid to the bottom of a hollow, and were soon buried under a wall of earth. During an attack you stumbled over a half-exposed arm or leg. Falling face to face on a corpse, you swore between your teeth — yours or the corpse's. Nasty the way these sneaky corpses would trip you up. But you took the opportunity to tear their identification tags off their necks so as to save those anonymous lumps of flesh from a future without memory, to restore them to official existence, as though the tragedy of the unknown soldier were to have lost not so much his life as his name. This no doubt was how Mathilde came to be notified that Emile

was dead and that his body lay somewhere in the Hauts-de-
Meuse sector. But what if Emile had lost his identification tag and someone else had picked it up? What if he
had exchanged tags with a buddy to further some secret
plan or to confuse an obtuse corporal? Could Emile really
be dead?

Prisoners returning from the ends of the earth, sometimes years after the war, kept hope alive. There were
stories about amnesiacs, real or feigned, who had begun a
new life somewhere in the East. In the blue eyes of a Polish
woman a penniless farmhand had found the few acres of
land that were not his in France. To the indigent, France
was less grateful than a lonely woman in need of strong
arms. Hungry soldiers, wandering about, were said to have
been rescued by enterprising matchmakers. A thick sand-
wich and a little warmth were sometimes enough to blunt
the homesickness of these tragedians in spite of themselves.
But why should Emile have gone elsewhere to look for what
he had here at home?

Mathilde's forlorn hope faded with the passing years.
For a time she found comfort in religion, not as her sister-
in-law would have wished, but in her own, more temporal
way, namely, friendship with an attractive priest. It would
be going too far to think of furtive embraces. At the most
they found pleasure in conversation, in embroidering together on the theme of their common loneliness —
affectionate banter that, like serene love, is sufficient unto
itself. After all, the Nazarene, too, was a handsome man; it
was women who defied the Sanhedrin and the law of Rome
and as a reward for their fidelity were the first to witness the
Resurrection. Paul of Tarsus wrote splendid letters that are
admired by all, but when the stammering midget turned up
in Ephesus or Corinth nobody wanted to listen to him.

Heaven had endowed Mathilde's priest with the face of an angel, which he made use of to bring stray sheep back to the fold. As a laborer of the first hour, Marie looked upon her erring sisters with Jacobin ferocity and took it out on Mathilde's petunias.

It took the letter from Commercy ten years to reach us. For Mathilde that letter marked the end of her youth, the moment of abdication when, though she might still allow herself to dream, she ceased to imagine that her dream could someday come true. Once the formulas of condolence reach us, we realize that none of the things we were hoping for will ever happen, that there will be no miracle, no sloe-eyed Polish woman getting her hooks into a chivalrous young Frenchman, no temporary amnesia — that Emile is really and truly dead. His buddy has written simply that he buried Emile in a makeshift grave at the foot of a eucalyptus tree and would be able to locate him if the family were interested in recovering the body; this seemed to have been his dying friend's desire and was the reason he himself had hidden the body — to avoid a mass burial or slow decomposition on the battlefield. After the first few lines Mathilde's eyes cloud over, her eyelids twitch, and tear after tear drops on the paper. Not that the letter was telling her anything new; she had known for twelve years that Emile was dead; what dismayed her was the finality of it, the end of her waiting, the door that had closed. She tots up the hours of happiness experienced in her lost youth, and the balance is so poor, so pathetic; so much grief for so little profit.

The winter of 1929 was one of the hardest on record. On February 2 a drunk was found frozen on his feet, leaning against a tree (*Le Courrier de l'Estuaire*). On the fifth, La Brière, the second largest marsh in France after the Camargue (formerly a bay dotted with islands, later filled in with alluvial deposits), froze solid in one night. Coypus, those raccoonlike rodents introduced into the marsh early in this century in the hope that the local population might derive some income from their fur, were found with half their bodies imprisoned in the ice after they tried to crawl out of their flooded burrows (*La Presqu'île de l'Ouest*). On the eighth, in the port of Saint-Nazaire, suddenly metamorphosed into Anchorage, a coastal steamer sank under the weight of the snow that had piled up on its deck. The docks and beaches were strewn with the corpses of gulls, white against white, heads tucked under wings in a last search for warmth. The Loire was clogged with drift ice, one block was so large that it almost sank a dredger near Saint-Florent — luckily the freshwater *Titanic* was saved by running aground on a sand bank. The whole country was paralyzed by snowdrifts. Trains were immobilized, and locomotives fitted with snowplows struggled to clear the tracks. As usual it was the poor who suffered most from nature's intemperance: beggars surprised by the white death at the bottom of a ditch or in makeshift shacks; isolated old people, sickly children, stray dogs and titmice.

It was under these polar conditions that Pierre set out in spite of Aline, who argued that he should wait for more propitious weather, considering that in his present situation

Emile was unlikely to fly away (we can imagine the stupefaction of the women who rushed to the tomb on that
Easter morning and instead of the body found only a little
pile of "linen wrappings" in the corner). After trying in vain
to work through administrative channels, Pierre had decided that he himself would go to the eucalyptus tree and
dig up his brother. Regardless of the weather, he was in no
mood to postpone his journey. But before going he made it
clear to Aline: it was a business trip, not a word to anyone
about its real purpose. And on the morning of the fifth, deaf
to her supplications, he set out for Commercy via the Loire
as far as Orléans, then continued eastward to Montargis,
Sens, Troyes, and Bar-le-Duc.

The handwriting on the back of the fine black-and-white
photo immortalizing the trip is Aline's, as can be seen from
her book of songs. Now that all danger is past, she notes
laconically, "February 5, 1929, departure for Commercy."
Pierre is at the wheel of an enormous car, almost a bus,
needed no doubt for his wholesale pottery business. The
driver's seat is on the right. Nothing English about it; simply that in those days people were more afraid of toppling
into the ditch than of what might be coming in the other
direction. Resting his elbow on the open window frame, his
face turned toward the photographer, he is visibly pleased
with himself, for he knows that cars like his are seldom
seen, especially in this town, where it may even be the only
one of its kind, suggesting a prosperous business —
altogether he has the look of a leading citizen with his
rimmed glasses and graying, slightly curled mustache. With
hat, coat, gloves, and scarf, he is armed against the cold.

Tall and wide, with a cloche pulled down over her ears,
Aline is standing beside the door. She has buried her face in
her little fox fur piece, which conceals her nose. There is a

certain elegance in her fitted coat. To fight the cold wind
that ruffles her fur, she rubs one leg against the other, with
the result that when the shutter clicks she is balanced on
one toe in defiance of the laws of gravity. She looks sad,
worried, disapproving, in contrast to Pierre with his childlike delight in his spiffy vehicle. She knows nothing can stop
him — and in that respect Joseph takes after his father. But
the son is absent from the picture. Maybe it was he who
held the camera.

"As I promised you, my dearest" — it is with these
words that Pierre opens his travel diary, and it is obvious
that his promise to give a faithful account was the price of
her permission to set out. He relates the most trifling inci-
dents of his journey: how he suffers from the cold and takes
advantage of every stop to warm his hands on the burning
hood of the car; how he encounters an irascible gas station
attendant; interprets a black cat crossing the road as an
omen of bad luck — and sure enough, the very next day,
somewhere in the Beauce or Brie region ("a white desert")
he swerves to avoid hitting a chicken, skids on the ice, and
ends up in the ditch. He thanks the two oxen that pull him
out and shares a bottle of wine with their peasant owner,
who with a grandiose gesture declines an offer of pay. This
diary is also an account book. Pierre is intent on showing
that this is no pleasure trip. He selects inns for the modesty
of their façades, his lunch consists of a quick snack, though
he grants himself a more substantial menu in the evening,
allowing us to choose as he does between pot-au-feu and
roast chicken. He enjoys the pot-au-feu but hastens to assure the reader that it doesn't come up to the incomparable
pot-au-feu he gets at home.

He drives carefully through the snow-covered countryside, recording the state of the roads, describing the chang-

ing landscape, noting the emergence of hedges and hills, commenting on the changing crops, the wooded regions — a quick course in geography. In Sens he waxes ecstatic over the cathedral of Saint Etienne, no doubt copying a description posted in the entrance, but such is his enthusiasm, one cannot help suspecting that its "majestic proportions" have put him in mind of the wife he has just left. When passing through towns he makes a note of hardware and home furnishings stores; now and then he steps into one of them (looking for ideas, so he says); at Troyes he expresses a poor opinion of the "painted stockings" that were then fashionable, classifies towns according to their degree of cleanliness. In the open country he notes variations in the light, a break in the clouds, the blue sheen of the hoarfrost, the diamond sheaths encasing the branches; blinded by all this whiteness, he pastes translucent colored candy wrappers on his glasses, and laughs at the sight of the clown in the rearview mirror. Taking pity on a tramp who has lost his way and is perishing with cold and hunger, he drives him to the nearest town and slips a few coins into his hand, but his feelings are much less charitable when a string of horse-drawn gypsy caravans forces him to drive at a snail's pace.

He thinks of his dead brothers, especially of the one whom he hopes to find under his eucalyptus tree, who will have held his little Rémi in his arms just once, and remembers what they went through together during that terrible war. He gives in to the temptation to detour by way of Verdun and stops at a small café-restaurant in Lemmes, on the *Voie sacrée,* where he finds survivors like himself, some unhurt, others hideously mutilated, communing with the same memories as he. All these pilgrims of pain, some of them German, recognize one another without a word and

nod their heads in greeting before sitting down. They are
unable to stay away from this scarred countryside, where
the symbolic value of their existence was so heightened that
it has never since had the same savor. The souvenir shop
near the café is kept by an amputee, who wouldn't complain about the loss of a leg if he had not also lost the
corresponding arm, which would have enabled him to use a
crutch. His wife deposits him there in the morning, and
there he waits bolt upright until she calls for him in the
evening. Feeling obliged to buy something, Pierre acquires,
for his sister, a few religious pictures printed during the
war. One of them comes from Commercy.

But most of his thoughts are for his wife, inchoate
thoughts, interspersed with words of tenderness, which find
their way into his diary as the distance between them in-
creases. Suddenly, at the bottom of a page written in a
dreary hotel room near Bar-le-Duc, we find his confession,
as fragile as a child's wish, that he misses her "infinitely."
The word, several times underlined, seems singularly apt,
as though the infinite could be measured only by the yard-
stick of that gigantic woman and as though her presence
sufficed to fill all the empty spaces in a man's life. And
thanks to that admission, we, along with the faded wallpaper of the room, the china water pitcher in its basin, and
the water bottle on the bedside table, share for a fleeting
moment in Pierre's immense desire for that ungainly
woman.

After that he hurries through the rest of his journey. He
stops dawdling, in his diary entries he abandons the fussy,
flowery style of the good pupil in favor of quick, ready-
made phrases, and no longer bothers to shape his letters.
His thoughts from now on are concentrated on his mission.
Of course the eucalyptus isn't there anymore; an incon-

gruity at that latitude, it died one winter after years of stubborn resistance; fortunately, its white stump is still recognizable, the writer of the letter can still find it and is merely surprised at having had to wait so long for an answer. After quick introductions, the buddy tells the story of Emile's last moments. Then the two of them, equipped with picks and shovels, go looking for the eucalyptus in the forest of Commercy. The muffled crunching of their footfalls in the snow.

The ground around the stump is frozen deep and solid. The strokes of the pickaxes echo through the forest. Shaken by the tremor, the branches of the trees nearby drop handfuls of white powder on the shoulders of the diggers. After hours of fruitless effort, they are forced to recognize that only a thaw can overcome the resistance of the ground. A thaw — that means when hens get teeth, and Pierre can't wait that long. But then Emile's buddy has an idea. They bring a washtub from his house, fill it with snow, heat it over a fire of dead branches, and pour the boiling water on the frozen ground. After a short wait they are able to dig into the hot mud and little by little, like cautious paleontologists, reach the body, which might be likened to a Grail. Pierre observes simply that it would be hard to recognize his brother in this vaguely human shape, decomposed by the acidity of the soil, the humidity, and the seasonal variations in temperature: tatters of jacket, intact belt buckle, scraps of skin barely covering the face and hands, the whole imprisoned in a sheath of frozen soil, no other way of extracting it than to pour a second tub of boiling water on these pathetic vestiges of life as upon a besieging army, with the result (when the cloud of steam over the excavation had dispersed, it was too late) that the last bits of flesh were removed by the seething magma. The veteran paleontologists now removed the bones one by one, completed the cleansing process by plunging them into the boiler, and laid them out in the snow in their approximate anatomical order. But then — horror of horrors! — they count more tibias than needed, two ribcages, and finally a second skull. Embarrassed by Pierre's look of consternation, Emile's buddy remembers that after digging the hole he noticed a second corpse that was rotting nearby and decided to bury it too. With all those bare bones divested of their last scraps of skin, the question arises: which of them belonged to Emile? Recalling that he and his brother wore the same size hat, Pierre attempts a desperate solution: he tries his hat on both heads. But the skulls have been so bruised and are so equally scalpless that Pierre puts his hat back on his head, after carefully wiping the sweatband. For a moment he is tempted to toss a coin (Simon de Montfort's system: God will recognize his own). As long as he has a complete skeleton . . . In the end he decides to take the one they dug up last, on the assumption that his brother must have been buried first. The letter writer was not so sure; perhaps, he reflected, he had started with the one that was more decomposed. At that point Pierre, fearing that too much juggling with possibilities might lead him to lose his brother's body, thinks it wise to hedge his bets and take them both.

They come back later with madeleine crates, which Emile's buddy, who works in a factory, expropriates for his rabbits. Coffins are unthinkable; every department Pierre passes through will demand a permit. And difficult as it would be to explain Emile's body, how could he possibly account for Emile's twin? They arrange the bones as best they can to keep them from rattling too much, pack them in straw like fragile crockery, load the crates into the car, and conceal them under a blanket. Mission accomplished,

Pierre starts for home without delay. In his hurry to get there he drives at high speed over snow-covered roads; time and again he narrowly escapes ending up in the ditch. He chooses secondary roads and avoids the larger towns, eluding detection thanks to the bad weather that keeps the police, along with almost everybody else, off the highways. He stops only to eat a quick bite, fill up his tank, sleep an hour or two by the side of the road, and, balancing his notebook on the edge of the steering wheel, to pen a telegraphic account of the exhumation. That is all we shall ever know about the last days of his journey. No one would hear about his breathless final spurt but the woman who made him hurry so.

When the family vault was opened upon the death of Mathilde, the grave digger was surprised to find those little ossuaries, plastered with advertisements for madeleines. But the grave digger was Yvon in his terminal state; it was child's play to convince him that in those days so many men died in the trenches that there were not enough boards for coffins.

IV

*O*N ALL SAINTS' DAY, 1940, Grandfather went to the cemetery with his daughter Marthe, whose first-born son lies under a bed of white gravel, a tiny Flying Dutchman sailing into the uncharted mists of the beyond, marked with an alabaster cross bearing at its center two sparrows' wings surmounted by a cherub's head. Under the November sky, as they make their way arm in arm down a side path bordered by Lilliputian graves, Grandfather points out a man showing a certain resemblance to Léon Blum, bent grief-stricken over a granite tombstone. A tall young man in glasses is trying to tear him away from the magnetic attraction of the flat stone. Whom, Grandfather asks his daughter, can the man be mourning? And Marthe, who knows everyone in Random, tells him about Aline, proprietress of the pottery shop next to the church, who died last summer: the softness of her voice, the tragedy of her stillborn children, her imposing stature and gold jaw. The grief-stricken man is her husband, the charming young man, the tallest among the mourners, is their son, Joseph, born after they had given up hoping for a child, and the frowning little white-haired lady, who hurries to join them, her head sunk between her shoulders, is the most extraordinary school-teacher in the Lower Loire department.

A year later, again at All Saints', the young man is alone beside the granite tomb. Léon Blum's double didn't lose any time, thinks Grandfather, amazed at the man's haste to join his wife. Years later, Grandfather would try to fathom the secret. He had collected the evidence in a shoe box: letters, photos, maps of the front, and the diary of Pierre's trip to

Commercy, that long confession of a husband to the
woman he had never left except during the war years, as
though the real purpose of his journey had been to get far
enough away from her to resume the tender correspon-
dence of the terrible years, to confess to her what can only
be confessed without confusion in writing, to recapture the
fresh emotion that comes of absence, to pile up distance so
as to rush back to her with new impetus. Secluded in his
attic, Grandfather digs up fossil traces of that attachment.
Time and again he turns over the photo of Pierre at the
front, in puttees and sky-blue uniform; his jacket stiff with
dirt, he holds his rifle by the barrel with the stock to the
ground; the lenses of his glasses are almost opaque, his
helmet on a slight slant that gives him an almost dandified
look but may have been produced by a push from a buddy.
Behind him, hanging from a peg driven into the trench wall,
a canteen and a grenade bag, and, in a little chapel-like
recess he has rigged up, a small Blessed Virgin — one suspects the hand of his sister Marie. In preparation for having
his picture taken, he has deposited his pipe on an improvised bench. From its bowl rises a thin fillet of smoke, a
signal unlikely to tell the enemy trench very much. Actually,
they too are smoking, writing to their families, cursing the
general staff, whose ruthless orders will soon fling them
into more misery and mud. The trench wall is barely higher
than he is. If he doesn't stick his nose out, he has nothing to
fear from snipers. He measures five foot seven and, according to his service record, which has also found its way into
the shoe box, has russet eyes. Russet? Seen through eyes of
that color, Grandfather reflects, all wives must have that
lovely, copper complexion that he himself was looking for
on the naked bodies of the women on the Ile du Levant.

Pierre smiles from the pit of horror. That is the best news

he can give. The addressee of that happiness is identified on the back of the photo: "To her whom I love so dearly." Grandfather turns the picture over and over, as though hoping to discover the mysterious bridge between front and back, between the tragic scene and the words of tenderness, as though the compound of love and death attested by the proximity of the dates on the granite tombstone were contained in the thickness of the card.

At the moment he sees the tall young man in mourning bent over the grave of his parents, the curve of his back coinciding with the curve of the cypress trees bent under the brisk November wind. He seems to be hesitating whether to lie down between them in the still-warm place of the miraculous child he was, as though already preparing to answer "Present" at the next roll call. His tall silhouette freezes in uncertainty between the crosses. The strength that has carried him thus far seems to have deserted him. Not yet twenty, an orphan, virtually penniless, war all around him — who would venture to choose for him? Little by little, the mourners leave the cemetery. Alone with the call of his entombed loved ones, insensible to the awkwardly affectionate tugs at his shoulders and to murmurs of encouragement, most of which, in view of the vanity of words, amount to no more than the repetition of his name. Aunt Marie comes up behind him, takes hold of his coat, pulls, persists, and finally prevails. All right, he'll keep trying. Accompanied by that stubborn strength, he makes his way up the central path — if only he were dead!

Translator's Notes

9 Lower Loire. Loire-Inférieure. In 1958, perhaps because the population regarded "inferior" as a reflection on their status, the department was renamed Loire-Atlantique. Similarly, Seine-Inférieure was renamed Seine-Maritime.

15 Saint-Nicolas. A church in Nantes.

18 nom de nom. Literally "name of name." Popular French has a number of "name of" exclamations: "name of a dog," "name of a pipe," etc., all euphemisms for "nom de Dieu," "name of God," an expletive ranging in tone and force from a genteel "goodness gracious" to something much more emphatic. "Nom de nom" is perhaps the most euphemistic of all.

20 La Jalousie du Barbouillé (The Clown's Jealousy). An Italian-style farce figuring in the repertory of Molière's troupe. It was formerly attributed to Molière.

20 Jansenist. Adherent of Jansenism, a theological doctrine based on the writings of the Dutch Roman Catholic theologian Cornelis Jansen (1585–1638) and holding with Saint Augustine that salvation was limited to a predestined few, the rest of mankind being doomed to perdition. Its best known supporter was Blaise Pascal (1623–62), the French scientist, mathematician, philosopher, and writer.

20 Chiffon. Le Mariage de Chiffon is a novel published in 1894 by Gyp, the pseudonym of Sibylle Gabrielle, comtesse de Martel de Janville (1850–1932), a prolific popular writer. Apparently an autobiographical work, since Chiffon was the writer's nickname.

31 sweep-up vans (voitures-balai). Jocose name given to the vans sent out to pick up participants in the famous bicycle race who had fallen by the wayside.

39 Saint Louis of the boules players. King Louis IX of France (1214–70) was famed not only for his religious fervor but also for his administration of justice. Sitting under an oak tree in the park of his château at Vincennes he judged disputes among his subjects.

40 *harkis.* Native Algerians formerly enrolled in units of the French army. When Algeria became independent in 1962, many were killed by Algerian revolutionaries. A few thousand were brought back to France with the army.

50 sprig of box. In parts of France where palm fronds were unavailable, sprigs of box, olive, or holly were carried on Palm Sunday.

51 *gave de Pau.* The mountain torrent near the Massabielle grotto, where the shepherd girl Bernadette had her vision of the Virgin Mary.

52 Monsieur Martin's daughter. Saint Theresa of Lisieux, born Thérèse Martin in Alençon.

52 Sulpician artist. A reference to the sentimental religious art radiating out into the Catholic world from the quarter of Paris surrounding the church of Saint-Sulpice.

53 Grand Albert. Both the Grand and the Petit Albert are cheap collections of popular magic, so called because they are attributed to the philosopher Albert the Great (Albertus Magnus), the teacher of Thomas Aquinas.

54 Saint Gourin. This appealing though apocryphal saint owes his existence to the charms of alliteration: *gare* = beware; *goret* = piglet; *se gourer* (slang) = to be mistaken.

63 *Très Riches Heures.* A reference to *Les Très Riches Heures du Duc de Berry*, a celebrated and beautiful illuminated manuscript begun in 1416 by the Limbourg brothers and completed in 1485 by Jean Colombe. The manuscript is now on display at the château of Chantilly near Paris.

69 Bobet. Louis Bobet, better known as Louison, born in 1925, won the Tour de France in 1953, 1954, and 1955 and was a popular hero in his day.

75 Grand Siècle (Great Century). A term rather inaccurately designating the reign of Louis XIV (1643–1715).

76 Wendels. The Wendel dynasty played a leading role in the French iron and steel industry from the early eighteenth century until the 1980s, when the government's nationalization program stripped it of most of its power.

78 Monsieur Séguin's goat. The heroine of Alphonse Daudet's story "La Chèvre de Monsieur Séguin," published in *Les Lettres de Mon Moulin* (1866), is a white goat who longs to be free, escapes to the mountains, and dies after fighting the wolf all night long.

97 Jansenist. See page 151.

97 Périer family. Pascal's sister Gilberte married the civil servant and physicist Florin Périer. The "charitable niece" was their daughter Marguerite, author of *Memoir on the Life of Monsieur Pascal.*

110 Pincevent. A village in the Seine-et-Marne department, not far from the site, discovered in 1964, of a large deposit of artifacts and human bones identified as a campsite of Paleolithic reindeer hunters.

110 Bach. Nom de guerre of Charles Pasquier (1882–1953), a "low" comedian specializing in crude military jokes and stories.

115 "La Paimpolaise." This song (words by Théodore Botrel, music by E. Feautrier), dedicated to the Iceland fishermen, was launched by Mayol in 1896 at the Concert Parisien. It is still popular, as are "Les Boeufs" ("The Oxen") by the poet and chansonnier Pierre Dupont (1821–71) and "La Petite Eglise" ("The Little Church") by the composer Paul Delmet (1862–1904).

118 newcomer who looks for Rome in Rome. "*Nouveau venu qui cherche Rome en Rome*" is the first line of a sonnet by the poet and humanist Joachim du Bellay (1522–60), deploring the passing of Rome's ancient glory.

121 Battle of the Thirty. In the course of the Breton War (1341–65) it was agreed that the fate of a certain fortified castle should be decided by a battle between thirty French and thirty English knights. As might be expected in a French historical legend, the French were victorious.

122 Nivelles, Schlieffen Plan versus Plan XVII. Alfred Graf von Schlieffen (1833–1913) was the chief of the German general staff from 1891 to 1906. His plan for defeating France by a massive flanking movement through the Low Countries was in the main taken over by his successor, Helmuth von Moltke (1848–1916), and was followed in the German offensive of 1914—which, however, spared Holland. The French, for their part, began preparing for war soon after the defeat of 1870. Between 1872 and 1914 no fewer than sixteen plans were considered by the French general staff. Plan No. 17, adopted on 15 April 1914, put more stress on offensive strategy than had previous plans and provided for measures to counter the eventuality of a German invasion of Belgium. Robert Nivelle (1857–1924) made his name while in command of the army at Verdun by recapturing a number of forts. Commander in chief from December 1916 to May 1917, he was

superseded when his Aisne offensive failed with enormous losses. His name has been widely associated with ruthless disregard for human life.

129 Clovis. Clovis I, old German Chlodwig (465–511), king of the Salian Franks, sometimes regarded as the first king of France, defeated the Romans at Tolbiacum (Zülpich), near the Rhine. The legend has it that a cross appeared to him in the sky during the battle. He was baptized soon thereafter.

129 Saint Geneviève. Saint Geneviève (422–512) is the patron saint of Paris. She assured the population that Attila the Hun would spare Paris, and it was widely believed that she had saved the city.

130 La Pérouse. Jean-François de Galoup, comte de La Pérouse (1741– 88), French navigator, explorer, and naval officer, distinguished himself in the war against England (1778–83) by destroying the forts of the Hudson's Bay Company.

133 Fontainebleau farewells (*les adieux de Fontainebleau*). In 1814, after his defeat at the battle of Leipzig, Napoleon abdicated in the château at Fontainebleau and bade farewell to his officers.

133 bees. The bee was the emblem of the Napoleonic Empire, replacing the fleur-de-lys of the old monarchy.

142 Simon de Montfort's system. Simon de Montfort, earl of Leicester (1208–65), was one of the principal commanders in the Albigensian Crusade. When the crusading army captured Béziers, one of his generals was reported to have asked him what to do about the population, since it included a large proportion of nonheretics. His answer: "Kill them all. God will recognize his own." These words may never have been spoken or may have been said by someone else. Be that as it may, some thirty thousand people were put to death.